Hour of Glory

Hour of Glory

Meditations on the Passion

GEORGE APPLETON

formerly Anglican Archbishop in Jerusalem

Darton, Longman and Todd
London

First published in Great Britain in 1985 by
Darton, Longman and Todd Ltd
89 Lillie Road, London SW6 1UD

Reprinted 1986

ISBN 0 232 51668 5

British Library Cataloguing in Publication Data

Appleton, George
  Hour of glory: meditations on the Passion.
  1. Jesus Christ—Passion—Devotional
  literature
  I. Title
  232.9′6   BT431
  ISBN 0–232–51668–5

Phototypeset by Input Typesetting Ltd London SW19 8DR
Printed and bound in Great Britain by
Anchor Brendon Ltd
Tiptree, Essex

Contents

Preface

Having lived in Jerusalem and visited the holy places on many occasions, I can echo the words of Steven Runciman from his *History of the Crusades*:[1]

> The desire to be a pilgrim is deeply rooted in human nature. To stand where those we reverence once stood, to see the very sites where they were born and toiled and died, gives us a feeling of mystic contact with them and is a practical expression of our homage. And if the great men of the world have their shrines to which their admirers come from afar, still more do men flock eagerly to those places where, they believe, the Divine has sanctified the earth.

This small book is a spiritual pilgrimage, beginning with the forty days Jesus spent in the wilderness, continuing through his ministry, culminating in the passion, and crowned by God's glorifying of his obedient and beloved Son in the resurrection.

It is a very personal book, addressed first of all to myself, as I have tried to re-create in imagination the gospel scenes, as if I were present, related them to my own life and times, and meditated in silence on the difference which these biblical narratives make to my own thinking, character and behaviour.

I have tried to bear in mind what all four evangelists have said, noting the additions which each has brought to his appreciation of Jesus, and any nuances that I had not perceived before. Readers will note that I have often quoted short biblical

[1] 3 vols. (Cambridge 1951, 1952, 1954).

passages verbatim, rather than being content with the references. I have done this because I am conscious of a temptation
in myself to skip looking up the actual passage.

I would emphasise to readers the importance of continuing
any meditation of mine by their own, for each of us has his or
her own background, personal experiences and needs.

Finally I would thank my publishers for entrusting to me
the happy task of undertaking these passion meditations, and
making them available for wider meditation.

Feast of the Transfiguration   + GEORGE APPLETON
    1985

Acknowledgements

Scriptural quotations are taken from either the Authorised Version of the Bible, Crown copyright, or from the Revised Standard Version of the Bible, copyrighted 1971 and 1952 by the Division of Christian Education of the National Council of the Churches of Christ in the USA.

1

Premonition of the Cross

The Christian pilgrim to Jerusalem and the Holy Land today
naturally tries to picture in imagination the life and ministry of
Jesus. To project oneself back through two thousand years of
history, through the destructions and rebuildings of the city
meant by God to be holy, and indeed sanctified by prophets
and supremely by Jesus, is not easy. The pilgrim, realising that
he is making the journey of a lifetime, wants to visit the places
where memories of Jesus still linger. He or she wants to crowd
into a week or two as many memories and experiences as the
travel agents, guides and spiritual conductors plan for each day.
There is little time to stand and stare, or search for significance
and meaning. It is easier in the quieter stretches of the shore
of Galilee or at Jacob's well in Nablus. I am often asked what
are the places where I experienced a sense of divine presence.
Jacob's well is one. The rock where Abraham was willing to
offer his most treasured son, which is now sheltered by the
golden mosque of Omar. A second rock, the rock of Gethsemane sheltered by the church of All Nations, recalls the victory
of the last night of our Lord's incarnate life. Another spot
where I felt compelled to stand in silence and reverence is the
place of entombment just inside the entrance of the great
church of the Resurrection, where Joseph of Arimathea, Nicodemus, the mother of Jesus, and the other Marys with John
the beloved and loving disciple, hurriedly anointed the body
with its five wounds and the brow pierced by the crown of
thorns, for the sabbath rest and the Passover festival.

There is another place where memory, sense of presence
and devotion combine to reduce the frequent visitor to longer

silence, less well-defined than the numinous places already mentioned – the wilderness countryside around the oasis of Jericho, where Jesus spent a great forty days after the spiritual experience of his baptism.

We give far too much prestige and initiative to the spirit of evil when we speak of this period as 'The Temptation'. Mark records, 'The Spirit immediately drove him out into the wilderness' (1:12), expressing a strong inner compulsion. He holds that Jesus was there for forty days 'tempted by Satan' (1:13). Matthew stresses a gentler divine initiative: 'Then Jesus was led up by the Spirit', but implies that the main motive was 'to be tempted by the devil' (4:1). Luke says, 'And Jesus, full of the Holy Spirit, returned from the Jordan, and was led by the Spirit for forty days in the wilderness, tempted by the devil' (4:1–2). John does not mention the forty days but reports the Baptist's description of Jesus as 'the Lamb of God, who takes away the sin of the world', and subsequent acts of Jesus to select a band of disciples, presumably to implement the guidance he had received after the experience of his baptism (1:36–51).

As I follow the first three evangelists in their accounts of the forty days lonely retreat of fasting and prayer, I come to the conclusion that the motive of Jesus was to find out from the mind of God how he was to fulfil his conviction of a special sonship, how to take away the sins of the world, and how to win the kingdoms of the world to become the kingdom of God. He had probably built for himself a small shelter of branches and palm leaves (cf. John 1:38), perhaps near the spring of fresh water at En-gedi.

I picture him sitting in meditation in that rustic booth or at points of vantage overlooking the Dead Sea, across to the mountains of what is now Jordan, or perhaps climbing the highest peak above Jericho from which he could glimpse Jerusalem and perhaps the Mediterranean, thinking of Athens and Rome; then looking eastward towards Persia and in imagination to India and China; and wondering how those kingdoms could learn of God's saving love and be brought under the rule of God. The gospels tell us of three possibilities that came into his mind. The flat round stones protruding from the sandy soil seemed like the flat loaves that can still be seen in the bazaars of old Jerusalem. He was hungry with fasting; should he use the power that had flowed into him at his baptism to provide food for himself and for the many hungry people in his own country and in countries of even greater need?

At first this seemed attractive, and without doubt he would have remembered how God had provided manna in Israel's liberating journey from Egypt to the land of divine promise and how Moses at its frontier had warned the first-chosen people that material prosperity would not in itself make a God-ruled and happy nation. Then a text from Deuteronomy was decisive: 'Man shall not live by bread alone, but by every word that proceeds from the mouth of God' (Matt. 4:4, Deut. 8:3). That is the priority for happiness and blessedness both for nations and individuals. So Jesus rejects the first possibility that comes to his mind. He will wait upon God in prayer and trust until a solution brings conviction. Material prosperity alone will not save humanity and usher in the kingdom of God, though he recognised that people must have food to eat and that the Father's will was that all should have abundant life.

It was perhaps a few days later that a further possibility suggested itself. Matthew and Luke differ in the order of possibilities, and Matthew's seems more likely. The suggestion comes, whether from God or the devil is not clear at first, that a sensational miracle might convince people and win them to God. Supposing he were to jump from a pinnacle of the temple, trusting to God to take him down safely? A verse from the Psalms comes to mind: 'He will give his angels charge of you. In their hands they will bear you up, lest you strike your foot against a stone' (91:11–12). Would not the crowds in the temple courts be impressed, believe in him and follow him to God? On the other hand, could not this be putting God to the test, demanding from him a proof of the spiritual revelation that had followed his baptism? Again the issue is decided by a reference to Scripture, once more from Deuteronomy, 'You shall not tempt the Lord your God', as the Israelites did in the desert (6:16). So this second possibility is seen to be a very subtle temptation.

Again there is a period of waiting, wondering and praying. The thoughts of Jesus go out beyond Israel and the temple, to the whole world. He is on Jericho's highest peak again, or in imagination picturing the farthest ends of the earth, the people of the nations and their rulers, for whom he feels a deep concern in his heart, whom he would bring into the kingdom of God's love. It may well be that he thought of Abraham and the hope that his descendants might bring a blessing to them all. How might he bring that vision and vocation to realisation? We are not told exactly what the third possibility was that occupied his attention. All that he would later disclose to his disciples, yet to be enlisted and trained, was that he saw in it the greatest and most subtle temptation of all. It suddenly seemed a compromise with world conquest, that if followed would amount to terrifying betrayal.

It may have been a possibility of winning the nations by force, as rulers of Assyria, Babylon, Egypt and Persia had dreamed of and almost succeeded in doing in the past, under all of whom Israel had suffered. He might have heard a whisper of some alliance with Rome, the contemporary world power, whose suzerainty extended over his country with governors, officers and troops ready to crush any rebels. Or the temptation might have been to ally himself with worldly and political ideas of messiahship. Whatever it was, Jesus saw that to follow such a course would amount to a compromise with evil, which had to be rejected. The rejection was immediate and total and once again comes in a text from Deuteronomy: 'You shall worship the Lord your God, and him only shall you serve' (6:13). So with authority, and a fierceness which denotes the strength of the temptation, the whisperer of evil is recognised and sent packing – 'Begone Satan!' Matthew in his account says that at this the devil left him, while Luke, hinting that there had been earlier and sustained attempts, says, 'And when the devil had ended every temptation, departed from him until an opportune time' (4:13). Matthew adds, 'behold angels came and ministered unto him' (4:11), as if to replenish his strength after a spiritually exhausting struggle.

What then did Jesus decide in that search for God's will and confrontation with spiritual evil? We are not told. We can only deduce the decision by studying the sequel in the gospel account of the ministry. From such a study it would seem clear that Jesus decided on the way of love, a vocation of service, a dedication to a ministry of sacrifice, which in all probability would lead to death. He could even in the earliest days see the shadow of a cross. Nothing less than death accepted willingly and wilfully would prove to human beings the infinite love in God's heart and in his own, and the limitless extent of divine forgiveness. It has been said that there was a cross in the heart of God before ever there was one on Calvary, caused by the sins, rebellions and refusals of saving love since men became rational, spiritual and responsible beings.

2

The Suffering Servant

Jesus had a detailed knowledge of the Hebrew Scriptures, which is all the more remarkable when we remember that all manuscripts had to be copied by hand. During the eighteen quiet years at Nazareth he must often have listened and talked to the local rabbi, who may have given him permission to take out the scrolls from the ark in the synagogue at Nazareth and study them. He knew the Book of Isaiah intimately, especially the later chapters which spoke of the Spirit of the Lord being upon the prophet and his call to be a light to the nations. There is embedded in these later chapters four poems which speak of a servant of the Lord, and are known as the Servant Songs. There are a number of direct quotations in the New Testament from these songs and a much greater number of references to them. Jesus says of himself, 'I am among you as one who serves' (Luke 22:27). Matthew's version is, 'The Son of man came not to be served but to serve and to give his life as a ransom for many' (20:28). The old priest Simeon is reported by Luke as taking the baby Jesus in his arms at the presentation and seeing him as a light to lighten the Gentiles. In the Book of the Acts, the first history book of the Church, Jesus is spoken of in prayer as 'thy holy servant Jesus' (4:27). In the Epistle to the Philippians Paul speaks of Jesus as 'taking the form of a servant', who 'humbled himself and became obedient unto death, even death on a cross' (2:7–8). Peter obviously knew the Servant Songs, for he speaks to Christians: 'by his wounds you have been healed. For you were straying like sheep, but have now returned to the Shepherd and Guardian of your souls' (1 Peter 2:24–5; echoing Isaiah 53:5–6).

So it would seem reasonable to believe that Jesus knew the four Servant Songs, meditated upon them during his forty days in the Jericho wilderness and made them the inspiration for his ministry. Christians in Lent and Holy Week meditate upon them in devotion and make them the pattern for discipleship. A few notes about their context and a paraphrase of their contents will help us both in devotion and discipleship.

The four songs are Isaiah 42:1–4, 49:1–6, 50:4–9, 52:13–53:12.

In the first poem God is represented as the speaker, describing his call to the servant, his endowment with the Spirit and the way in which he will carry out his servanthood:

Look at my trusted servant whom I uphold; my chosen one in whom I delight. I have endowed him like the prophets with my spirit and he shall proclaim true religion to the nations. He shall not be loud and noisy, worked up in a frenzy like the professional seers. He shall not crush a broken reed nor quench the dimly-burning wick. He shall faithfully set forth true religion. He shall not grow feeble or discouraged until he has set true religion in the earth, till far-off lands long for his revelation.

In the second song the servant himself tells of his call, his feeling that he has failed, yet his continued trust in God. He hears God telling him that his call is to a far wider mission than to Israel. He is to be a light to all the nations, and his message is to reach to the farthest ends of the earth.

Listen to me distant lands and far-off nations. The Lord called me from my earliest days to be his servant. He has given me a penetrating message to cut through pretence and opposition. He has made me like a swift straight arrow and stored me in his quiver for a special purpose, telling me that he will use me for his glory. I thought that I had laboured in vain and exhausted my strength with no result. 'But surely', I said, 'the Lord will do me justice and reward my efforts.'

And the Lord who called me from my birth to bring back Israel to him now says to me, "Tis too light a thing to bring the survivors of the exile safely back home. You shall be a light to the nations, and through you my salvation shall reach the ends of the world.'

In the third song, again the servant is the speaker, telling how every morning the Lord God has spoken within him, and he has been obedient to the divine instruction. He tells also of growing opposition and shameful treatment, in the face of which he trusts in God to vindicate him and confound all those who insult and oppose him.

The Lord God has given me the tongue of a disciple so that instructed by him I may know how to answer the godless. Every morning he draws me into communion with him, and I have never disobeyed, nor let cruelty or insult make me shrink from the tasks he has given me. I know that the Lord will help me, so I shall not be overwhelmed. I set my face like a flint, confident that I shall not be put to shame. He will make it clear that I am right, and all my adversaries shall perish like a moth-eaten garment.

In the last of the four songs the servant is dead. The Lord promises that he will not have lived in vain and that even the rulers of the nations will come to interpret his life and death in a true way, and marvel at God's vindication of him. Through his obedience, suffering and death, the servant will have won forgiveness and blessing for many.

Behold, my servant shall succeed and shall be raised to such a glorious position that nations shall do him homage and kings be reverently silent in his presence, gazing at the wonderful transformation that has taken place. 'Whoever could have believed what we had heard,' they cry, 'whoever could have seen the Lord's power so clearly revealed? We thought of him as a sapling growing in unpromising soil, with nothing attractive about him. He was a man who had borne pain and sickness, so despised and shunned by others that we thought him to be of no account.

'But now we recognise that it was our pains and sicknesses that he bore, though we thought him smitten by God as a punishment for his sins. Yet he was wounded for our sins and cursed for our misdeeds; he suffered chastisement to bring us prosperity and healing.

'We had all gone astray like sheep, each going his own way, and the Lord had allowed our guilt to light on him.

'He was ill-treated but he accepted it humbly and never complained, as innocent as a lamb being led to the slaughter, as defenceless as a sheep in the hand of the shearers. They did away with him unjustly and who heeded how he fell, struck down by sins of ours? They buried him with criminals despite his life of innocence and his complete devotion to truth.

'But the Lord chose to vindicate him, rescuing his life from failure. Because he gave his life as an offering for the sins of others, he shall see spiritual descendants carrying on his work and God's good will shall be accomplished through him. He shall recognise that all his sufferings were spiritual birth pangs and shall be fully satisfied in what has been brought to birth.'

Yes indeed, says the Lord, my righteous servant has suffered that many should be brought to righteousness through his obedience.

Because he shed his life-blood and was willing to be numbered with rebels, bearing the sins of men and interceding for them, therefore shall he win victory and triumph gloriously.

The Lord always vindicates those who try to be his true servants.

The writer of these four lovely poems which so inspired Jesus does not name the servant, and there has been much discussion of whom he might have been. Some biblical scholars have thought that he could have been Jeremiah, and certainly as we read the Book of Jeremiah, we see the sufferings of a sensitive spirit in the face of insult, rejection and cruel treatment. The writers of the New Testament confidently believe that Jesus deliberately fulfilled the vocation of the servant, and that his life and passion have won forgiveness for the sins of the world. There is a vivid little parable in Luke's Gospel which shows our Lord's determination to serve: 'Will any one of you, who has a servant plowing or keeping sheep, say to him when he has come in from the field, "Come at once and sit down at table"?' This is just what our Lord is always doing, and is what each perceptive and loving Christian will be on the look-out to do. I think of the effect on a housewife, tired with a day's cleaning and cooking, if her husband or son or daughter says, 'Sit down my dear, you look tired out, let me get you a nice cup of tea.'

George Herbert may well have had this one-verse parable in mind when he wrote:

Love bade me welcome; yet my soul drew back,
    Guilty of dust and sin.
But quick-ey'd Love, observing me grow slack
    From my first entrance in,
Drew nearer to me, sweetly questioning
    If I lack'd any thing.

'A guest', I answer'd, 'worthy to be here.'
    Love said, 'You shall be he.'
'I the unkind, ungrateful? Ah my dear,
    I cannot look on thee.'
Love took my hand, and smiling did reply,
    'Who made the eyes but I?'

'Truth Lord, but I have marr'd them; let my shame
    Go where it doth deserve.'
'And know you not', says Love, 'who bore the blame?'
    'My dear, then I will serve.'
'You must sit down', says Love, 'and taste my meat.'
    So I did sit and eat.

As we read the full biblical passages or the paraphrases I have attempted for my own devotion and imitation, we note that in several mentions the servant stands for Israel, oppressed by powerful nations, and this is sadly true of the Christian centuries, where often the Church has been active in persecution of the Jews or acquiescent in it. Clearly the Church is meant by its master to be a servant community, in obedience to God and in service to the neighbourhoods in which it worships and works. Every parish, congregation and synod ought from time to time to consider in what ways it can serve society, not only in charitable care, but in the creation of right attitudes towards human problems and the dispositions of the individual spirit which bring peace of heart and victorious living, as well as provide a leavening and reconciling influence.

The individual Christian cannot fail to see in the four songs a pattern for his or her own discipleship and servanthood. I am called and meant to be an embodiment of the servant. It would be good for me to read through these four songs regularly, as spoken to or by myself, to see if I live up to them, and what modification or extension may be demanded in the changing conditions of my own life or of the life going on around me.

In the concluding verse of the fourth Servant Song, the prophet hears God lay down the conditions of spiritual effectiveness: 'Therefore I will divide him a portion with the great, and he shall divide the spoil with the strong; because he poured out his soul to death, and was numbered with the transgressors; yet he bore the sin of many, and made intercession for the transgressors' (Isaiah 53:12). If I am to be a servant like the servant of the four Servant Songs, I must be ready to pour out my soul unto death, to hold nothing back even if it means death or until the last moment of my physical life. Secondly, I must be ready to identify myself with the sinners or oppressors, feeling with them, taking my stand with them, as Jesus did at the Jordan ford where the Baptist was preaching. Thirdly, I must bear the sins of others on my heart, not just condemn them, but to feel the sinfulness and tragedy of them, the damage that those sins are doing to the sinner himself as well as to those against whom they are done, in short to feel the awful solidarity of sin.

Lastly, I must be ready to make intercession for the transgressors, as Jesus did in his first word from the cross, not only praying for their forgiveness, but even finding excuse for them. Intercession is essentially the prayer of love and concern, in which we offer ourselves to be channels of his grace and healing. Most of us find it easier to pray for those in trouble, illness, misfortune and disaster, than to pray for those who defraud or injure us, for criminals and terrorists, and even with such rebels and predators to pray for them generally rather than for individuals who have harmed us. Such people are sick in spirit and so only spiritual cleansing and healing can save them. If I am to be a servant of Christ, the perfect servant of God, I must learn to pray as he did and still does.

The writer of the Epistle to the Hebrews sums up the fourth Servant Song, particularly in its use of the adjective 'suffering' in another single verse: 'For it became him for whom are all things, and by whom are all things, in bringing many sons unto glory, to make the captain of their salvation perfect through suffering.' It was only through Christ's experience of every aspect of human life, including suffering, that he reveals to us that he was completely human, and only by doing so could he become the captain of our salvation, the healer and saviour of us all, those of us living today, those who lived our life in our world in the past, and all yet to be born.

So we come back in reverent imagination to our Lord in the pregnant and determinative first forty days of his ministry. We picture him in the Jericho countryside, patiently working out how he will carry out his call, ministry and sonship, and bear on his heart the dreadful sins of humanity, and by his cross and passion redeem the world, and show to people of every generation God's saving love, and the pain and longing in the Sacred Heart, until the last lost son and daughter come back to the Father, who is not only our Creator but our merciful and loving Saviour.

3

The Lamb of God

In the biblical account of Abraham and the boy Isaac journeying to the rock of sacrifice on Mt Moriah, later incorporated into the sacred precincts of the temple, there is a very moving moment when Isaac says to his father, 'My father, behold the fire and the wood; but where is the lamb for a burnt offering?' Abraham's heart must have been deeply wounded at this childish question. He is not yet ready to tell him of the plan in his mind, so he replies somewhat evasively, 'God will provide himself the lamb for the burnt offering, my son' (Gen. 22:6–8). One often notes that in the Bible something said in a seemingly ordinary situation has within it a deeper interpretation which only becomes clear much later. God did provide a lamb who would be an eternal and universal sacrifice, willingly offered for the sins of the whole world.

John the Baptist, convinced that he was sent to prepare the way for a Coming One, was taken aback when his cousin Jesus, at the end of a day's baptism of many conscience-stricken people, stood before him at the Jordan ford. The fiery preacher of judgment knew that this last applicant for baptism was different from all the others, and so he hesitated but finally agreed. Jesus was identifying himself with those whom he watched in this symbolic mass baptism. Perhaps he had heard their faltering confession of sins. By the time that Jesus returned from his fasting retreat forty days later, John knew that the Coming One who would baptise with the Holy Spirit as well as with water had come. So he pointed out Jesus to two of his own disciples, John and Andrew, with the words, 'Behold, the Lamb of God, who takes away the sin of the world!' The two followed Jesus and became the first of the twelve, representing the twelve tribes, who were to go out to the whole world with a gospel of forgiveness and love (John 1:29–39).

Mark in his Gospel says that on the first day of Unleavened Bread when the lambs were killed in preparation for the Passover, Jesus made secret preparations for observing the festival. John differs from the three other evangelists in saying that Jesus was crucified on the day before the Passover, on the day the lambs were killed. If this was so, Christian devotion would see an identification of Jesus with the Passover lamb, offered in commemoration of the liberation from slavery in Egypt, and now offering himself to liberate people from the slavery of sin: 'Christ, our paschal lamb, has been sacrificed. Let us, therefore, celebrate the festival' (1 Cor. 5:7). There is a further symbolism in that the Passover lamb was to be without blemish, not disabled in any way, a fact that John noted when at the crucifixion our Lord was pierced by a spear to the heart, rather than having his legs broken, as in the case of the two men crucified with him (19:32–6).

It is in the Book of Revelation that the symbolism of the lamb is even more elaborated. A scroll is seen which no one can open and John weeps about the failure and is consoled by an elder who tells him that 'the Lion of Judah' will succeed in doing so (5:1–5). Then John sees a Lamb, bearing marks which show that it has been slain but is now living, who takes the scroll from the hand of God to open it. This is a remarkable change of imagery from a martial one of power symbolised by a lion, to the gentle image of a lamb, which may signify the writer's conviction of the change brought about by Christ. The four living creatures and the twenty-four elders now burst into song:

Worthy art thou to take the scroll and to open its seals [to reveal the divine message], for thou wast slain and by thy blood didst ransom men for God from every tribe and tongue and people and nation, and hast made them a kingdom and priests to our God.

Myriads take up the anthem saying, 'To him who sits upon the throne and to the Lamb be blessing and honour and glory and might for ever and ever' (5:6–13). The Lamb shares the worth of God, and worship is offered to him as well as to God.

So the crucified, risen and glorified Christ is hailed as 'The Lamb who has ransomed men for God and made them into a royal house of priests in God's service' (see also 1:5–6). Later, John sees 'a great multitude which no man could number standing before the throne and the Lamb, clothed in white robes made white through the death of the Lamb, guided to springs of living water, with the promise that God will wipe away all tears from their eyes' (7:9–17).

We may be puzzled at a first mention of 'the wrath of the Lamb'. This is not an attribute of the glorified Christ, in John's thinking, nor does it represent the personal attitude of God towards sinners, but 'is the working out in history of the conse-quences of the rejection and crucifixion of the Messiah'.[1] People are always free to accept the forgiveness and salvation of God; rejection brings certain consequences in its train. As John says in his Gospel, 'God sent the Son into the world not to condemn the world, but that the world might be saved through him' (3:17).

It is the confident conclusion of the Book of Revelation that 'The kingdom of this world has become the kingdom of our Lord and of his Christ, and he shall reign for ever and ever' (11:15). We may see here the true answer to the third possibility which was so urgently desired by our Lord in the forty days in the wilderness, which we thought about in Chapter 1, and in which he rejected any compromise in loyalty. Also we gratefully keep in memory John's mention of the Lamb's book of life in which the names of those who are saved are written, with the

---

[1] A. T. Hanson, *The Wrath of the Lamb* (London 1957), pp. 159–80.

hope that the names of those not yet there will by the loving mercy of God and their acceptance of it be added.

That all may be saved if they will is envisaged in John's final vision of the City of God with its twelve gates inscribed with the names of the twelve tribes, and its twelve foundations inscribed with the names of the twelve apostles of the Lamb, illuminated by the lamp of the Lamb, with the nations streaming into it bringing their spiritual treasure, and the gates never shut in the eternal day.

The Church in its liturgy enshrines its faith in the Lamb of God, both in the Gloria and in the Agnus Dei with its threefold prayer for mercy and its praise for the salvation won for us by the Lamb, and in its Sanctus, where we join with the angels, saints and holy souls made perfect in the worship of heaven.

The Lamb wins forgiveness not only for the grievous and habitual sins of individual sinners, but also for the corporate sins of mankind, the solidarity of the world's sinfulness, the sins of nations, political, economic and social groups, a nuclear infection of both evil aggression and retaliation. Every age needs forgiveness for its wrong values, for its greed and materialism: in our age for the growth of terrorism; the devaluation of human life, the tragic falling standards in truth, justice, righteousness and honesty; and the misuse of modern technology always liable to cancel out its positive benefits; for hooliganism which spreads as rapidly as fear in a bush fire; selfish nationalisms which fail to move towards the unity of mankind; and a failure in compassion and helpfulness to the nations whom we euphemistically speak of as 'developing'.

It is not easy for nations to repent for things committed in the past or for one generation to feel responsible for the sins of an earlier generation. Our Jewish friends, for example, find it difficult to forgive the Christian Church for centuries of wrong treatment and acquiescence or even involvement in persecution, or the German nation for the Nazi atrocities before and during the Second World War, which we speak of as the Holocaust. The British Council of Churches is engaged in a three-year study project entitled, 'Forgiveness and Politics', which may yield insights and inspiration. One may wonder how we would feel in the grief and feelings of a Jewish friend who as a small girl was in a concentration camp and saw her mother kicked on the ground by a Nazi guard before being herded with many others into the gas chamber.

Perhaps the answer to the problem of national guilt and mutual forgiveness is solved when a sufficient number of people in one nation feel that some episode in the past is to be regretted, or some policy and relationship in the present be changed. It does not require that everyone in a nation should agree, for Jesus taught us in a parable that a little yeast leavens the whole lump of dough. A Hindu friend suggested that even as small a percentage as ten could effect a change, if the spiritual yeast kept its leavening quality. Jesus also said to his first disciples that they were to be as salt (Mark 9:50); only a sprinkle can flavour a whole potful or preserve certain food from going bad.

An example of this possibility of forgiveness comes to mind. Shortly after it was decided that Burma should attain independence five leading members of the Governor's executive council were assassinated, including the popular Prime Minister-designate, General Aung San. A rival politician, U Saw, was suspected, arrested, found guilty and hanged. The Anglican Bishop George West, talking with U Nu who became the national leader, asked if U Saw had confessed to the crime, and was told that he had not, U Nu adding, 'If he had done so, we would not have hanged him.'

Another incident comes back in memory. During the trial of Adolf Eichman, a Nazi criminal who was kidnapped and brought to Israel, I happened to meet the publisher Victor Gollancz; and when asked what he thought should happen, his reply was that he believed that Eichman would certainly be found guilty, but he hoped that he would be set free, presumably with the mark of Cain upon him for the rest of his life. That might not amount to forgiveness, but it would surely be a step in the right direction.

Perhaps the question of group forgiveness can best be

answered by thinking in terms of reconciliation. Paul in his Second Letter to the Christians at Corinth says, 'God through Christ reconciled us to himself and entrusted to us the ministry of reconciliation. So we are ambassadors for Christ, God making his appeal through us. We beseech you through Christ, be reconciled to God' (2 Cor. 5:19–20). Paul is thinking primarily of reconciliation to God, but that implies reconciliation with men too.

The New Testament also speaks of Christ as bearer of our sins. No one in the history of salvation has felt the tragedy and sinfulness of sin as he did. He bore on his heart the sins of individuals and of human beings as a whole. He recognised the damage that sin does to those whom God has created and loves and so he is eternally opposed to sin. He must in some sense be opposed to us as long as we continue in sin, but with sorrow, compassion and longing that we should accept his forgiveness. Most Christians would probably say that God forgives as soon as we repent, but some would believe, as I do, that he forgives before we repent and that it is his forgiveness that softens our hearts and moves us to penitence. Perhaps it is nearer the truth to say that the divine forgiveness can only be effective in us when we begin to hate evil and sin as he does. Paul encourages this thought when he says in his Letter to the Romans, 'Why, one will hardly die for a righteous man – though perhaps for a good man one will dare even to die. But God shows his love for us in that while we were yet sinners Christ died for us.' (5:7–8)

One of the happiest phrases in the New Testament is that used by Luke of a woman who had been living an immoral life, 'a woman who had been a sinner' until she encountered Jesus. Something in him touched her heart, a holiness yet accompanied by compassion and love, which elicited from him the assurance, 'I tell you, her sins which are many, are forgiven, for she loved much' (7:47). All down the ages since that day, the saints who have been drawn nearest to God are conscious of the gap between them and the God of holiness and love. He who was called 'the Lamb of God' indeed takes away the sins of the world: he did so in the gospel days, he does so still, and will do so in the future, until every poor sinner has had the opportunity of seeing the holy and righteous God embodied in his Christ.

4

Acceptance of the Cross

Throughout his ministry Jesus had a foreboding how it would all end, but it was not a foreboding from which he wanted to escape. There was with it an inner conviction that it would and should be right, that the Father with whom he was so intimate and whose will was always good, loving and wise, would ensure that somehow it contained a positive intention and a promise of good.

We saw in Chapter 1 the intuitions that came to him in the forty days following his baptism, inner urgings that the way to move people's hearts was not through force or magical miracles or a legalistic adherence to system, but through service, sacrifice and love which could ultimately lead to shame and death, if in circumstances which might arise that should appear to be the will of God. The future beyond that would be in the hands of God. His knowledge of God made him sure that trust was the only way; acceptance, not reluctant but even joyful, would lead to a God-inspired and God-controlled future. The last word would always be with God.

At several significant moments in his ministry Jesus was confirmed in his belief that suffering and death would be the climax. At Caesarea Philippi, after Peter's leap of faith in him as the Messiah, Matthew records: 'From that time Jesus began to show his disciples that he must go to Jerusalem and suffer many things of the elders and chief priests, and be killed, and on the third day be raised.' This was evidently something new to the twelve, particularly to Peter, who now exclaims, 'God forbid, Lord! This shall never happen to you', only to be rebuked, in the most severe rebuke in the whole of the gospels,

'Get behind me, Satan! You are a hindrance to me; for you are not on the side of God, but of men' (16:21–3). Peter must have been taken aback and hurt. Jesus must have felt that the same temptation was coming to him again as he had experienced and repelled in the forty days in the wilderness.

A similar occasion was on the night of the transfiguration. Luke tells us that the two spiritual beings, Moses and Elijah, 'spoke to him of the departure he was to accomplish at Jerusalem' (9:30–1). As Jesus and the three disciples come down from Mt Tabor, he commands them to say nothing about the vision until he is raised from the dead. They then question him about the popular idea that Elijah must come first, to which Jesus replies that 'Elijah has already come, and they did not know him, but did to him whatever they pleased. So also the Son of man will suffer at their hands' (Matt. 17:12).

On the final journey up to Jerusalem he warns his disciples that everything in the prophets which he has accepted both as vocation and fulfilment will be accomplished. Jesus becomes more explicit: 'For he will be delivered to the Gentiles, and will be mocked and shamefully treated and spat upon, they will scourge him and kill him, and on the third day he will rise again' (Luke 18:32–3). Luke adds a verse showing the puzzlement of the disciples: 'But they understood none of these things; this saying was hid from their eyes and they did not grasp what was said.' It is possible that writing forty years later the evangelist feels able to include exact details of what happened which were not as explicit at the time when Jesus spoke.

Mark, whose account of this incident Luke follows almost word for word, gives a picture of Jesus purposefully striding ahead, and the disciples following, apprehensive both for him and themselves also: 'And they were on the road, going up to Jerusalem, and Jesus was walking ahead of them; and they were amazed, and those who followed were afraid' (10:32), which may have been a memory told to Mark by his uncle Peter when they were in Rome together.

Jesus was always insistent on consulting the Father at every step, and not acting until he was sure that the right moment had come. At the wedding in Cana of Galilee, when his mother whispered to him that the wine had given out, he answered, 'My hour has not yet come' (John 2:1–4). A few minutes later it had come. In the meantime he had consulted the Father and was clear that his mother's implied advice was right. On another occasion his 'brothers' had announced that they were going up to Jerusalem for the feast of Tabernacles and expected him to accompany them and to seize the opportunity of speaking openly to the world. He had replied that their time was always at their disposal, but his time had not yet fully come. A few days later he judged that his time had come, and we can surmise that in the meantime he had prayed to the Father, perhaps not about the comparatively small matter of accompanying his brothers on the journey, but on the crucially important issue of speaking openly to the world about his mission from God (John 7:1–10).

In the week before his arrest Jesus took precautions not to fall prematurely into the hands of the Jerusalem authorities (John 11:54), but as the Passover festival drew near he said, 'The hour has come for the Son of man to be glorified'. On the night before he was arrested John records that 'Jesus knew that his hour had come to depart out of this world to the Father' (12:23, 13:1). Always the initiative and the decision were with Jesus. A little earlier he had made this abundantly clear: 'No one takes my life from me, but I lay it down of my own accord. I have power to lay it down, and I have power to take it again: this charge I have received from my Father' (John 10:17–18).

Jesus was in no way an eccentric, unworldly, good-natured man falling into the hands of fanatical, unscrupulous enemies; he was the strong man taking his challenge into the territory of his opponents at a moment determined by himself, dependent only on the will and guidance of the Father.

Nor did Jesus accept the cross reluctantly or in a spirit of resignation in which he had little or no choice. The writer of the Epistle to the Hebrews says of him, 'who for the joy that was set before him endured the cross, despising the shame' (12:2); and quoting Psalm 40:8, 'I have come to do thy will, O my God . . . I delight to do it, for thy law is within my heart' (Heb. 10:7). The joy is because he is sure that the cross is God's will, and anything that God wills must be accepted with joy. In the parish church of Stepney, where I served as a curate, there is now a stained-glass window which depicts Jesus as a young man with a smile on his face as he hangs upon the cross.

James his 'brother', whatever that means, says that we his disciples should welcome similar trials, 'Count it all joy, my brethren, when you meet various trials, for you know that the testing of your faith produces steadfastness' (Jas 1:2–4).

It may well be asked, 'In what way was the cross God's will?' Could it possibly have been God's original, perfect will? The teaching of Jesus in the gospels is that the Father's will is always right, loving and wise. Yet that divine will must be related to the actions of men and their reactions to him. His purpose in Christ was to reveal his love, to save them from sin, and in the event of their sinning to assure them of forgiveness. Jesus was to do all this whatever the reaction of men: if they were to reject him, if they were to oppose and persecute him, even if they were to kill him, he was to continue loving them. This is exactly what Jesus did.

By continuing in sin men were to alienate themselves from God. Paul says that 'God was in Christ reconciling the world to himself, not counting their trespasses against them' (2 Cor. 5:19).

At certain times in the past people have thought of God as a stern and guilt-exposing Being who demanded a sacrifice, which was offered by the gentle and loving Jesus as the price of forgiving. People who thought in that way in the past or think so now, forget those gracious promises of the gospels – 'God so loved the world that he gave his only Son', 'God sent the Son into the world, not to condemn the world, but that the world might be saved' (John 3:16–17). 'You shall call his name Jesus for he shall save his people from their sins' (Matt. 1:21).

Luke in his Gospel puts together three of the saving parables of Jesus – the lost sheep, the lost coin and the lost son – three ways of getting lost and found, which between them cover a much greater number of people. All three parables speak of the joy of the figure representing God, and the joy in heaven over even one sinner who returns to the Father's home.

There are people who think that whatever happens, good or evil, is caused to happen by God, in spite of the teaching of Jesus that God alone is perfectly good. Such a view can only be even slightly credible in that all that is good is willed and wrought by God, but that man is free to reject or oppose it, and he does so as the negative response to God's positive good. Much of the evil and suffering in the world is the consequence of man's wrong ideas and behaviour, rather than God's angry punishment. Nor is there any room to believe that the future is inexorably fixed. Paul as well as the Buddha taught that as a man sows so shall he reap. There is a harvest of deeds, good actions producing happiness and blessing, evil deeds the opposites. 'By their fruits you shall know them,' said Jesus, both in men as well as trees. We cannot possibly believe that God wills or causes cancer, hunger, disease, hijacking, concentration camps, torture chambers, death by violence, mental illness, premature death. These things happen against his will, through men's ignorance and fear, through sinfulness and selfishness, individual, social or natural, and also through wrong ways of living, worry, over-work, over-eating, through intoxication and drug addiction. The gospel asserts that in every case God is at work to heal, redeem and save, and abounding grace is available for every sin and tragedy.

People in suffering often say, 'What have I done that God should do this to me?' the gentle answer to which is twofold: 'My dear, God has not done it, and he is always at work to bring good out of it.' There are different ways of dealing with tragedy and misfortune. We can let it knock us out, we can become bitter and rebel against it, we can fill our lives with frantic action in an attempt to forget, or we can accept it in trust that tomorrow God will make clear to us what is so difficult to understand today.

So there is an acceptance on our part, taking Christ as our exemplar, endeavouring to grow into his spiritual stature, and believing with his great interpreter Paul, that 'the whole creation has been groaning in travail [birth pangs] until now' and that creation waits with eager longing for the revealing of the children of God, to use it in the Creator's way, as Paul says in Romans, Chapter 8 (21–2), which he ends with a triumphant declaration of faith:

> Who shall separate us from the love of Christ? Shall tribulations, or distress, or persecution, or famine, or nakedness, or peril, or sword? . . . No in all these things we are more than conquerors through him who loved us. For I am sure that neither death, nor life, nor angels, nor principalities, nor things present, nor things to come, nor powers, nor height, nor depth, nor anything else in all creation, will be able to separate us from the love of God in Christ Jesus our Lord. (Rom. 8:35–6, 38–9)

The cross and the resurrection are the evidence that this is always so, as joyfully for us, as those two greatest experiences were for Jesus.

5

The Week of the Cross

During the last week in the incarnate life of Jesus things happened very quickly, one happening after another increasing the sense of danger and threat of death. The enmity of the authorities, the precautions of the Roman occupying power, the determination of Jesus to choose the right moment of the Father's will. Mark tells us of the growing threat: 'The chief priests and the scribes were seeking how to arrest him by stealth and kill him; for they said, "Not during the feast, lest there be a tumult of the people" ' (14:1–2), evidence that Jesus was respected and admired by a large number of people, and also evidence of how mistaken Christians have been in forever holding the whole Jewish race guilty of the death of Jesus. It looks as if Jesus, as well as the chief priests and their friends, saw the approaching Passover festival as a key moment, which would be the right time to give himself into their hands, for the crowds in Jerusalem, including Jesus, would be from many countries, and greater than at any other time in the year. He, rather than the priests or the Roman authorities, would be deciding the date of his death.

Let us examine the days of the last week and see the mounting tension and danger in the tussle of initiatives and will: Jesus knew that there would be a large number of pilgrims from Galilee, many of whom had listened to his preaching on the shore of the lake, possibly had even spoken to him, who spoke from his heart to their hearts about God's love and forgiveness. So he waits for them at Bethany in the home of his friends Lazarus, Martha and Mary.

The last time he had been with them, the two sisters had

been in great grief over what had happened to their brother. Jesus had restored him to life and had spoken words of comfort, authority and promise which have brought hope to people of every generation since, and will go on doing so as long as this world lasts. A supper is arranged in his honour. Reading John's Gospel it looks as if the supper was not in the house of these three intimate friends of Jesus. Martha however is busy as usual with preparation and serving. Lazarus is also a guest sitting close to Jesus and naturally attracting special attention. Mary, with gratitude for her brother's restoration to life, and also in personal gratitude to Jesus for his influence in her life, brings a cruse of costly ointment and anoints the feet of Jesus, and wipes his feet with her hair, an act of grateful love. The evangelist says that the whole house was fragrant with the scent of the ointment. It may have been the kind of ointment used in the embalming of dead bodies.

Jesus, by this time conscious that the death he is expecting is near and that the right moment for it is coinciding, interprets Mary's tribute of love as an anticipatory anointing of his dead body. Judas regards Mary's act as wasteful; the expense might have been used for the relief of the poor. John, who much later, writing this memory and the part of Judas in handing over Jesus to the authorities, is still critical of Judas, remembers our Lord's acceptance of Mary's devotion and his association of it with the Jewish duty of the care for the dead, which for the moment death comes is superior even to the care of the poor. Only someone who had been present on this occasion would have remembered the somewhat enigmatic word with which Jesus concludes the incident – 'The poor you always have with you, but you do not always have me' (12:8). Any gesture of grateful and gracious tribute to Jesus need not conflict with the perennial duty of almsgiving and caring for the poor. However it is the association of Mary's act with our Lord's expectation of death that lingers in the mind and arouses our anxious apprehension of what is approaching.

While he is there he arranges with a friend for the loan of a donkey with a foal, who agrees to lend him the two animals whenever he sends for them. The Galilee crowd arrives and probably camps out there, after a tiring last trek. They may even have rested there for what would be the last sabbath Jesus would enjoy before his death. The day after the symbolic anointing he prepares his plan, the donkey and foal are borrowed as arranged. The twelve disciples who all believe that Jesus is the Messiah, and the pilgrims from Galilee who hope that he is, co-operate in an enthusiastic entry into Jerusalem. Branches of palm are cut down and waved, garments are spread on the road for the donkey and its foal. Some of the crowd go in front of Jesus, others follow, and all shout joyfully, 'Hosanna! Blessed is he who comes in the name of the Lord! Hosanna in the highest!' (Mark 11:9–10). There is no doubt about the messianic cheers of the pilgrims as they approach Jerusalem. The disciples go ahead of their Master, believing that the great day of the Lord, longed for alike by prophets and people for centuries, has come at last.

Jesus cannot but have been touched by their joy and loyalty. He has already planned his own response, in the choice of the donkey on which to ride, meant to remind people of a text from the Book of Zechariah (9:9) and of his own interpretation of messiahship: 'Tell the daughter of Zion, behold, your king is coming to you, humble, and mounted on an ass, and on a colt, the foal of an ass.' Not on a war horse surrounded by troops will he enter the holy city, not as a conqueror in robes of state, but riding on a donkey, the animal of peace and everyday usefulness; not received by the leading men of Jerusalem but accompanied by a crowd of ordinary people.

John's Gospel tells us of a crowd of pilgrims who came out from Jerusalem to welcome him, shouting the same messianic greeting. Many, doubtless, were curious to see this popular teacher from Galilee, many may have hoped, like the disciples, that he would liberate their country from Roman occupation and fulfil the promises of their Scriptures. Only the authorities frowned disapprovingly and remarked to one another, 'You see that you can do nothing, look, the world has gone after him' (John 12:19). Their intention, however, remained the same. Indeed they had already warned their supporters, as John (11:57) records: 'Now the chief priests and the Pharisees had given orders that if anyone knew where he was, he should let them know, that they might arrest him.'

The route taken by the triumphant procession from Bethany was not the gently rising road to Jerusalem taken by pilgrims today, but one over the brow of the Mount of Olives, which almost suddenly comes upon a wonderful view of the walled city across the Kidron valley, with the temple precincts, as it were, spread out before the eyes, surrounded by the houses and caravanserai for travellers. At this point Luke tells us that Jesus stopped, gazed at the view and burst into tears: 'And when he drew near and saw the city he wept over it saying, "Would that even today you knew the things that make for peace! But now they are hid from your eyes." ' He went on to warn that war and destruction would certainly come, 'because you did not know the time of your visitation' (19:41–4).

Matthew includes an even more moving lament over Jerusalem in his account of our Lord's condemnation of the scribes and Pharisees: 'O Jerusalem, Jerusalem, killing the prophets and stoning them who are sent to you! How often would I have gathered your children together as a hen gathers her brood under her wings, and you would not!' (23:37). Both laments show the love of Jesus for Jerusalem, his grief at its lack of holiness, its rejection of himself, and his warnings of inevitable disaster.

Arrived in Jerusalem, Jesus goes immediately to the temple, 'my Father's house', as he had called it on his first visit as a boy some twenty years earlier. Whether it was on that evening or the next day that he cleansed the temple is not quite clear. Mark and Matthew, however, agree that he was moved to indignation at the irreverent ways in which it was being used, people treating it as a short-cut, overcharging by those who sold the things needed for sacrifices or by the moneychangers who supplied Jewish money for the temple tax and offerings. Things must have been very bad for Jesus to infer that it had become a den of thieves, instead of a house of prayer for all nations. We can well imagine the scene as Jesus overturned the tables of the moneychangers, released the lambs and doves, and in his indignation driving those in charge out of the temple. No wonder that later the authorities asked him by what authority he was doing these things. Their determination to get rid of him hardened still further.

On the following day Jesus is back in the temple preaching openly to the people in its courts. Pharisees and Sadducees attempt to discredit him in the presence of the many people listening eagerly to him or to trap him into saying something which would get him into trouble with the occupying power. Others, perhaps less hostile, ask about his warning that the temple will itself be destroyed unless there is a drastic change in both church and nation. Still others ask about the end of the world, and are told that only God knows the day when this will happen. To all he urges the need of watchfulness, so that they may live in such a way that when this happens they are not unprepared. He illustrates this as always with vivid parables – the wise and foolish bridesmaids, the employer giving his servants money to use on his behalf while he is away and calling them to account on his return. One particular parable shows that he is aware of the danger ahead: the tenants of a vineyard refuse to pay the absentee owner his agreed share of the grape harvest, they ill-treat his messengers, so he decides to send his much-loved son and they even kill him.

In another parable Jesus pictures all the nations gathered before the Judge of all, who divides them into two great groups in the same way that a shepherd divides the sheep from the goats. The sheep on his right hand the king admits into the eternal kingdom that has been prepared from the beginning, for they have fed the hungry, clothed the naked, cared for the sick and visited those in prison, and the king accepts these works of mercy as if done to himself. The goats on his left hand are consigned to punishment, on the same principle that in refusing or neglecting to help those in need, they have refused help to himself. This parable in Matthew 25:31–46 needs to be studied in our contemporary situation, when there are so many nations living comfortably, even luxuriously, and at the same time other nations suffering in desperate hunger and widespread disease, unable to rescue themselves. We are told by UN experts that if every nation, rich and poor, gave 0·7 of 1 per cent of its national income, world poverty could be banished in a generation. Great Britain gives less than half of this necessary percentage. The crucified Master and risen Lord will continue to accuse and reproach us every Holy Week until this is done, and will regard what we do or what we do not do, as done or not done to himself. It is not the gracious act of gratitude done by Mary Magdalene, it is the duty to love our neighbour as ourselves, a command repeated by Jesus only a day or two before his expected and accepted death. It is his last will and testament, and we his disciples are his appointed heirs and executors.

6

Gentiles at the Passover

'Now among those who went up to worship at the feast were some Greeks' (John 12:20). The visit of these Greeks from Galilee is the only incident which John records between the entry into Jerusalem and the Last Supper. They were not Greek-speaking Jews, but probably God-seeking and God-reverencing men, attracted by the Jewish religion with its central message of faith in God and admiring the ethical character of Judaism. Possibly they attended worship in the synagogue on the sabbath, as we are told in the Acts happened in many of the centres which Paul visited in the course of his three missionary tours.

There were a considerable number of them living in the Decapolis area south of the lake of Galilee. They would have heard of the prophet of Galilee with his message that the great time longed for by the prophets was near, and his insistence that God was a God of love, not one of condemnation but of forgiveness and saving love. So they seek out Philip, whose home town was Bethsaida, just north of the lake. Philip is a Greek name and that may also have been a reason for approaching him. Their request to him is, 'Sir, we wish to see Jesus' (12:21). Philip consults Andrew, whose name is also Greek rather than Hebrew. Together they go to tell Jesus.

The first response of Jesus is one of exaltation, 'The hour has come for the Son of man to be glorified' (12:23). A seed has fallen into the earth and germinated, perhaps an unexpected seed. In his reply Jesus uses the term 'Son of man', a more general phrase than 'Son of David', embracing Gentile as well as Jew. These Greeks are to Jesus, and to John as he writes his Gospel, representatives of the Gentile world.

John tells us that this feeling of exaltation is followed almost immediately by one of tension, 'Now is my soul troubled' (12:27). For the moment, Jesus does not know what to say or what to pray.

As happened in the beginning of the ministry when he was thinking of how to win the world for God, and as almost every time an inspiration of duty and loving service comes into our minds, a spirit of evil or dark shadow, as the psychologists call it, creeps in in the wake of what we believe came from God. It knows that with Jesus it is no good prompting him to something clearly and blatantly evil, so it suggests some way of distorting and deflecting the God-given intuition, which may at first seem right and good, but which will result in defeating the divine will.

In the case of Jesus the entirely good thing is in ensuring that the wider world gets the salvation God intends for it. The possibility of the gospel-message being more warmly welcomed in the world outside was an attractive one. So why not go outside Israel whose authorities were rejecting him and plotting to kill him? The dark shadow in it could well have been a subtle evasion of the cross, the same temptation that Jesus would experience several days later in Gethsemane. The same thought had been in the mind of the hostile critics of Jesus, when he spoke to them openly of going away somewhere where their malice could not reach him: 'The [Jerusalem] Jews said to one another, "where does this man intend to go that we shall not find him? Does he intend to go the Dispersion among the Greeks and teach the Greeks?" ' (7:35). The idea was not a new one when the Greeks from Galilee asked to meet him.

The time, however, must be right, God's time, not his own time, and certainly not the time of other people. So, as always, he consults the Father in prayer. At the opening of his prayer he does not know what to ask. Shall it be, 'Father save me from this hour', not the hour of decision, but the hour of suffering which up to now he has accepted as the Father's will?

The answer seems to come at once – No! he must not pray that prayer. Then what shall he pray? The second answer comes equally quickly, 'Father, glorify thy name' (12:28). Within his spirit the answer comes from God, 'I have glorified it, and I will glorify it again.' There is an external, equally mysterious sound, which needs interpreting – a clap of thunder. Some of the crowd, perhaps superstitiously, think that God spoke in the thunder. Others more biblically inclined say that an angel spoke to him (12:29), for many Jews, perhaps more then than now, believed that messages from God are brought by angels, divine messengers.

In his teaching in Galilee Jesus often told parables about the kingdom of Heaven being in many ways like a seed. Here he refers to the fact that a seed must fall into the earth and die, before it germinates, grows and finally bears fruit (12:24). In nature unless the seed dies it cannot grow into a root of corn, a tree bearing fruit every year or a plant producing a number of flowers. So without his death there cannot be a harvest of the spirit, love, joy, peace and the other virtues.

He goes on to say that the passion signifies the 'Judgment of the world', the overthrow of evil, glory being shown in his death, and the assurance of the drawing of all people to himself. The final decisive and faith-convincing word is, 'I, when I am lifted up from the earth, will draw all men to myself'. John makes quite clear that this saying refers to crucifixion, an agonising form of execution which only the occupying Romans could pass sentence for and carry out, and not death by stoning which would be a Jewish sentence, or a death by mob violence (12:32–3).

Those hostile in the crowd now bring up another argument: the Scriptures and law both assert that the Messiah when he comes will remain for ever, and Jesus if he is executed cannot therefore be the Christ. In any case, they ask, 'Who is this Son of man' of whom you are so often talking and claiming to be? Jesus replies that he has come to bring God's light to them, and appeals to them to walk in that light while they have the opportunity. There is a danger that they will refuse the light, and the consequence of that will be a real darkness in which they will grope hopelessly and helplessly.

As today we meditate on this incident, we find embedded in it a message for ourselves: 'he who loves his life loses it, and he who hates his life in this world will keep it for eternal life' (12:25). Jesus was a teacher who did not hesitate to use hyperbole (exaggeration) to bring home the meaning and importance of his message. God, he tells his hearers, is glorified by complete obedience in his servants, and those who do not desire their own will but only the will of God who sent Jesus most truly glorify him. On the other hand, to hate one's own life is to regard it as of secondary importance compared to the duty, joy and reward of putting God's will first completely and always.

It is interesting to note that Matthew includes in his account of the birth of Jesus the meaningful story of the wise men from the East who came in search of a universal God and Saviour. Their offerings of gold and incense signify the wealth and worship of the nations, and a third offering of myrrh is symbolic of death and embalming. The old priest Simeon, who presided at the presentation of the baby Jesus in the temple, took him in his arms and blessed God, mystically seeing in the child the fulfilment of Isaiah's hope of a light to lighten the nations. So throughout the gospels Jesus had the world in his heart, and therefore the God that sent him to reveal the divine nature and will equally loves the world and wants all people in every generation to come into that saving love. John's perceptive comment, when he recorded the encounter with Nicodemus on a certain evening in Jerusalem, is still in his mind as he writes of the meeting with the Greeks in the outer court of the Temple two or three days before the crucifixion – 'God so loved the world that he gave his only Son' (3:16). The Son so loved God and the world that he was ready to give his life to prove that message true.

7

The Last Supper

Jesus alone knew where he and the twelve disciples were to keep the Passover. He had kept it secret even from his most intimate friends. Possibly he had noticed the occasional absence of Judas, and did not want him to know lest he should inform the authorities, who wanted to arrest him. If this should happen he would not be able to give them his final instructions nor do certain other things he had in mind. At some time previously he had secretly arranged with a friend where he hoped to celebrate the Passover.

So on the day when the Passover lambs were killed ready for the festival, the disciples asked where they should prepare. Luke tells us that he then sent Peter and John at a fixed time, telling them that at a certain gate of the city they would see the unusual sight of a man bearing a pitcher of water, whom they were to follow. When he arrived at his house they were to say to him, 'The Master says, "where is the guest room, where I am to eat the Passover with my disciples?" ' Evidently the man was a friend whom Jesus trusted and who regarded him as Master. So Peter and John did as Jesus had instructed them and there prepared for the supper (22:7–13).

Towards nightfall Jesus and the rest of the twelve joined them. Luke tells us that on the way a dispute arose among them as to who should be the greatest in the kingdom; their worldly ideas of the Messiah had evidently been revived by the triumphal entry a few days earlier. Perhaps none of them was ready to bring water and a towel for the customary feet-washing before entering a house. Jesus tells them that in the kingdom of God worldly standards are reversed and the greatest is the one who serves rather than the one who is served, a point he had stressed when some weeks earlier James and John had made a request that they should sit on either side of him in his glory. The remaining ten must have had similar ambitions for they were indignant at the two brothers.

To drive home his point Jesus himself takes a bowl of water and girds himself with a towel and kneels at the feet of each in turn, and washes and dries their feet. As he does this, looking up into the face of each the memory may have come to him of his first meeting and in a flash the story of his relationship with each. He would know the strength and weakness of each one and what was still lacking before each became the kind of person that the Master wanted him to become. It must have been a poignant moment for Jesus and a disturbing moment for Judas when Jesus looked into his eyes, wonderingly and reproachfully. Peter at first refuses to have his feet washed, feeling that what is happening is the wrong way round and that he ought to be washing the feet of Jesus. The Lord says to him, 'If I do not wash you, you have no part with me', whereupon Peter in his usual impulsive way says, 'Lord, not my feet only but also my hands and my head'. Again there is a gentle reproach: 'He who has bathed is clean all over and does not need to wash, and you are clean', and then, 'but not all of you', a signal which Judas alone would recognise (John 13:1–11).

They then move to the supper which has been prepared, not yet the Passover meal, according to John, who dates the crucifixion differently to the other three gospels. Luke rather supports John's dating, for he records Jesus saying to them, 'I have earnestly desired to eat this Passover with you before I suffer; for I tell you that I shall not eat it again until it is fulfilled in the kingdom of God' (22:15–16).

As they sit or recline round the low table, Jesus thanks the disciples for their faithfulness to him: 'You are those who have continued with me in my trials; as my Father appointed a kingdom for me, so do I appoint for you that you may eat and drink at my table in my kingdom and sit on thrones judging the twelve tribes of Israel' (Luke 22:28–30). He has shared with them his understanding of God's kingdom, so they will be able to judge whether or not the twelve tribes have qualified for membership in it.

John tells us that Jesus adds that those who receive them will also be accepting himself who has sent them. It looks as if he is giving them a last commission to carry on his work. But his heart is heavy that one of them does not share his understanding of the kingdom and is already planning to hand him over to the authorities. They are dismayed when he tells them this and one after another anxiously ask, 'Lord, is it I?' 'Is it I?' . . . 'Is it I?' Even to ask such a question is to show a basic loyalty, each questioner being worried lest unwittingly he should have been disloyal. It looks as if all through the early part of the evening Jesus is letting Judas know what is afoot and even appealing to him not to do what he is planning. Jesus adds that when he discovers his mistake and the consequences of it he will wish that he had never been born.

The others are loud in their protestations of loyalty, and Peter adds vehemently, 'Even though they all fall away, I will not!' (Mark 14:29). Jesus warns him that that very night he will deny him. Luke in his Gospel includes a memory that he has picked up in his research into the facts of our Lord's ministry: 'Simon, Simon, behold Satan demanded to have you that he might sift you like wheat, but I have prayed for you that your faith may not fail, and when you have turned again, strengthen your brethren' (22:31–2).

It is a moving thought that Jesus with all on his mind was praying for Peter. Some will feel that he was praying too for Judas and the others. What he did in his incarnate life he will have continued to do in his risen ascended life, and as we shall see in his high-priestly prayer, for all who have come to know him through the witness of his disciples. The writer of the Epistle to the Hebrews, whose aim was to show Jewish Christians how Jesus fulfilled the highest hopes of Judaism and at the same time interpret Jesus to those Jews who did not accept him as the Christ, says of him, 'He is able for all time to save those who draw near to God through him, since he always lives to make intercession for them' (7:25). So the individual Christian today can be both comforted and grateful for the assurance that the ever-living Christ knows the circumstances of each and prays for each, though as he later said to his first disciples, 'I do not say to you that I will pray to the Father for you, for the Father himself loves you, because you have loved me and have believed that I came from the Father' (John 16:26–7).

Let us go back to the disciples troubled at the disclosure of Jesus that one of them will betray him and that he knows who it is. Peter leans across to John who is reclining next to Jesus and asks him to find out who it is. Jesus replies that it is the one to whom he will give a piece of unleavened bread dipped in the common dish, ordinarily a gesture of honour and affection. Then he gives the dipped morsel to Judas. It is possible that John did not pass this identification on to Peter, knowing that Peter would probably do something to defend Jesus, as he was to do in the garden of Gethsemane. We are also told by Luke that there were two swords with the company in the upper room (22:38) and that would explain how Peter had one to hand when Jesus was arrested.

One can imagine that Jesus looked very intently and appealingly at Judas when he passed the morsel from the dish, adding so that no one else would guess the significance, 'What you are going to do, do quickly.' Possibly he realised that nothing was going to alter Judas's plan. Judas then rises from the table and goes out quickly. Writing years later, John closes this incident with the terse words, 'And it was night', in more senses than one (13:21–30).

We are not told explicitly whether the Judas incident came before or after the way of remembrance which Jesus gave to his disciples, by far the most memorable of all that took place that night in the upper room. At some time during the supper Jesus took bread, and having said over it the usual blessing of God, he broke it and gave it to them, saying, 'This is my body which is for you, do this in remembrance of me'. In the same way he took a cup of wine, saying, 'This cup is the new covenant in my blood. Do this as often as you drink it in remembrance of me.' The new covenant was that expected by Jeremiah (31:31), when all should know the Lord, who would forgive their sin and remember it no more.

The accounts in Matthew, Mark and Luke differ in detail. The Church in its eucharistic remembrance has followed Paul's account of the institution in 1 Corinthians 11:23–6, which is considerably earlier than that of the three evangelists. John does not include an account of the institution; he has in Chapter 6 much longer passages, interpreting its spiritual meaning.

Some scholars have thought that what was celebrated in the upper room was the Khiddush, a ceremony performed on the eve of the sabbath and great festivals. In this, after the mother has lit the sabbath candles, the father in the family takes a loaf, says over it a blessing of God, and breaks the loaf into small pieces, which he distributes to everyone present. He then takes a bottle of wine and says over that also a blessing of God, and pours a small portion into little cups, and all drink. This ceremony is still performed today in Jewish families and other groups. Jesus knew that his disciples would meet in this way on sabbath and festival eves, and so he attached to it a regular remembrance, which his disciples faithfully observed. In time as they did so, they experienced a nourishment of the spirit and a sense of the presence of the risen Lord, which Christians today believe and experience in the Eucharist.

There were other things to note in that last evening together. There was the giving of the new commandment: 'A new commandment I give to you, that you love one another; even as I have loved you, that you also love one another. By this all men will know that you are my disciples, if you have love for one another' (John 13:34–5). From now on the criterion of love is no longer the commandment to love our neighbour as ourselves, but the command to love one another as Christ has loved us, something far more costly and deep and universal.

There follow three chapters (John 14–16), in which Jesus sets out the meaning of what is going to happen, and the memories that are to guide them in the future. First of all he tells them plainly that he is going to the Father. This will be expedient for them and result in greater things than he has done in his incarnate life, for he will be with the Father, and the Father is omnipresent in his creation. The Son will be omnipresent with the Father, no longer tied to one place, and no longer under the domination of time, and physical presence. So their hearts are not to be troubled.

Then Jesus promises them that he will return to them, 'in a little while'. They will see him again but the world will not, hinting that they will then have a different kind of sight, and their spiritual eyes will be opened. The 'little while' is surely the time between his death and the time when they see him in his risen life.

A third theme in these discourses in the upper room is the relationship between Jesus himself and the disciples, as close as the relationship between the vine and its branches, which will enable them to bear spiritual fruit, just as the connection between the branches and the main stock on which they grow organically results in clusters of grapes. No longer does Jesus call them servants, they are his friends, for he has shared with them all that he has learnt from the Father. Moreover he leaves them a legacy of peace, a much deeper and richer peace than the things of the world can give. So they are to abide in him and let him abide in them.

He warns them that they cannot expect any different treatment from the world than that which he has received. If they belong to Christ the world will hate them, for Christ has chosen them out of the world. So they must expect to be excluded from the synagogue, people will even claim that in killing them they are doing God a service.

However, to enable them to endure all this, he will send a Strengthener, a Comforter, a Counsellor, an Enabler, who will guide them into all truth. This Spirit will cause them to remember the things that Christ has taught them, and bring out their deeper meaning. It is not easy for the student of the fourth gospel to distinguish between the actions of Jesus and the actions of the Spirit. That is not to be wondered at, for the nature and being, and will and action of God are a mystery, and a joyful mystery, to the human mind. Even the writers of the New Testament share this co–inherence, sometimes speaking of the Spirit of God, the Spirit of Jesus and the Holy Spirit.

It may well be that Jesus himself understood this difficulty, for he said to those first disciples, 'I have yet many things to say to you, but you cannot bear them now'. In those words there is hope and promise of growing maturity, as Paul wrote to the Christians at Corinth: 'When the perfect is come, the imperfect will pass away . . . Now I know in part: then I shall understand fully, even as I have been fully understood' (1 Cor. 13:10, 12). All this, however, will not compare with the joy of seeing God face to face.

Jesus has said to them all that is in his mind. His final word still shows his apprehension on their behalf, but he concludes, 'Be of good cheer, I have overcome the world', with the implicit promise that they too, similarly, will overcome all the forces against them. As they stand around him before leaving the upper room, he pours out his heart to God for them in a prayer which Christians have called the great high-priestly prayer.

8

The First Victory

Chapter 17 of John's Gospel is for Christians one of the greatest chapters of the whole Bible. Any meditation on it should be preceded by a thoughtful reading, with silences for the promised Spirit to reveal new depths and personal relevance.

John remembers how Jesus stood with his eyes lifted to heaven, with the same joy in his face as they had seen when they had watched him in rapt communion with the Father. The prayer falls into three parts: first of all a spirit of thankfulness for all the Father has done already; secondly a prayer for his present disciples; and lastly a prayer for later believers. In the first part he recognises that the hour has come for which he has been waiting, so he prays that the Father will glorify him, so that he may continue to glorify God. He is clear that he has been entrusted with the task of giving eternal life, the Father's quality of life and his own, to the whole human race. He is implicitly thankful that he has been shown the secret of eternal life – 'To know Thee the only true God' – not just to know about God, but to know God personally, in spirit and in truth. It would seem that John added, 'and Jesus Christ whom Thou hast sent', a supposition which would be entirely true when one remembers the emphasis which Jesus has made all through John's Gospel on his identity with the Father.

In the second part (17:6–19) Jesus says that at this stage he is not praying for the world, but for the disciples whom God has given him, though we shall see as the prayer proceeds that the world is always in his heart. So he prays: 'Holy Father, keep them in thy Name.' Keep them true to the revelation I have given them.

He goes on to pray that 'they may be one, even as we are', that is, with the unity that has always existed between the Father and himself, a mysterious, deep and complete unity. He assures the Father that he has lost none of the first disciples, except 'the son of perdition [destruction]', one who has destroyed himself.

He goes on to pray, 'that they may have my joy fulfilled in themselves', the joy of sharing the divine life, the joy of doing the divine will, and the joy of suffering brought about by obedience to the divine will.

He does not pray that they should be taken out of the world, for he is sending them into the world, just as the Father has sent him. So he prays that the Father will 'keep them from the evil one'.

He finally prays, 'Sanctify them in thy truth', that they may consecrate themselves, just as he has consecrated himself. They are to be priests to the world.

Jesus then goes on to pray for those who will believe in him through their witness, that they too may be one, so that the world may believe. He prays that they may be perfectly one, with the same unity that exists between him and the Father, and that they may be with him and see the glory in the mutual love which goes back to eternity, before the world came into being. He knows that the world does not yet know the Father, but that these first disciples have learnt to love the Father through him, and that he himself may be in them and they in him, thus reinforcing the mutual indwelling of which he had already spoken, of himself as the vine and them as fruit-bearing branches. If throughout the divided churches today there was deeper desire for the divine indwelling and more prayer for it, not only during an annual week of prayer for Christian unity, but throughout the whole year, the unity of God's will would soon come and the way to achieve it would be shown to us. Christian unity is the price all individual Christians and all the churches have to be ready to pay. We cannot expect humanity to become one, until the Church is one. 'That the world may believe' is the recurring and ultimate aim of our Lord's great prayer. It must be ours also. Otherwise we are not his true disciples.

Having prayed that prayer, Jesus leaves the upper room and with the eleven descends into the Kidron valley to the garden of Gethsemane, a place where he often went for prayer, and a place which Judas knew, should he and the authorities not find him in the upper room.

Arrived there, he asks them all to pray, and taking Peter, James and John with him, he tells them, 'My soul is very sorrowful even unto death; remain here and watch with me. And going a little farther he fell on his face and prayed' (Mark 14:34–5; Matt. 26:39). Luke adds, 'And being in an agony he prayed more earnestly; and his sweat became like great drops of blood falling on the ground' (22:44). We Christians talk about the agony in the garden. People who do not know the origin of the phrase talk about 'sweating blood', when they are facing some danger that may end in death.

The evangelists tell us what Jesus prayed. Mark words it, 'Abba, Father, all things are possible to thee; remove this cup from me. Yet not what I will, but what thou wilt' (14:36), using the intimate word for 'Father' which Jewish children used then and still do, one of the actual Hebrew words preserved in our English versions of the gospels, and one which we might often use, for it has the intimate, loving sense of 'Father, dear Father'.

We who try to enter into our Lord's anguished prayer in Gethsemane may well believe that he was now facing the immediate certainty of death. As fully human as we are, he shrank from the long physical agony of crucifixion and the finality of death. Humanly speaking, death would be the end of all his hopes, it could even be termed failure. Could that possibly be the Father's will? That was what he wanted to find out. So he repeatedly prays, 'Father, if it be possible, let this cup pass'; the cup he had talked about a short time previously, to James and John and their mother, and the rest of the disciples; 'Can you drink the cup I have to drink?' 'Can I, must I, drink it?' Luke tells us that an angel from heaven came to strengthen him, a way of saying that his prayer was being answered. So now he adds to his prayer, 'Nevertheless, not my will, but thine be done.' If the cross is really God's will it must be done, for, as he has so often preached, God's will is always good, always loving, always wise, and if followed will turn out to be effective, the best thing that could possibly happen, even or indeed especially in the worst of circumstances.

Jesus is completely human, as we are, in another way. He needs and values human companionship and sympathy. So three times he comes to the three trusted companions, only to find them sleeping. He wakens them and reproachfully asks, 'Could you not watch with me one hour?' He has a special reproach for Peter, who an hour or so earlier had sworn his loyalty: 'Even though they all fall away, I will not . . . if I must die with you, I will not deny you.'

Waking them the third time, Jesus suddenly breaks off with the words, 'Rise, let us be going; see, my betrayer is at hand.' He has heard and seen the party of temple police, accompanied by Pharisees and chief priests and a crowd of others with swords and clubs, coming through the olive trees, and at the head of them, Judas Iscariot!

The first great battle of the cross has been won, within the heart and mind of Jesus. He has faced the certainty of excruciating pain, he has put aside all human thinking. As in the retreat in the desert at the beginning of his ministry he has decided that obedience to God is primary, he has kept his love for the world undiminished, and above all has affirmed his complete trust in God to see him through the cross, and has gladly handed over responsibilities for the future to the Father. The first fierce battle is over, and he can march on with trust and peace in his heart to the last and fiercest strife which is only a few hours ahead.

John does not tell us of the agony in Gethsemane, but he gives us a vivid account of the arrest. Jesus with calm dignity goes forward to meet the advancing crowd, and asks, 'Whom do you seek?' They reply, 'Jesus of Nazareth', and when he tells them, 'I am he', John says they fall to the ground in surprise. Perhaps at this point Judas, as arranged with the chief priests, as reported by the other three evangelists, comes forward and kisses Jesus. Both he and they want to be sure not to arrest the wrong man in the darkness of the olive trees, the night only lit up by the flaming torches.

Jesus does not refuse the kiss, and indeed it may have been a kiss of wayward affection in the misinterpretation of Judas, who wanted to force the hand of Jesus into exerting both authority and force. Matthew records Jesus as saying, 'Friend, why are you here?' (26:50); Luke puts it: 'Judas, would you betray the Son of man with a kiss?' (22:48). Whatever the motive in Judas's mind, whether gross misunderstanding of his Master, or downright treachery, in the mind of Jesus it amounted to betrayal. It is interesting to note that in our Lord's last words to Judas, he uses the term 'Son of man' with its messianic undertone.

One of the disciples, unnamed in Matthew's account (26:51) but identified as Peter by John (18:10–11), now attempts a one-man rescue. Taking a sword he begins to slash out right and left, only to be peremptorily rebuked by Jesus. 'No more of this!' Matthew adds,

> Put your sword back into its place; for all who take the sword will perish by the sword. Do you think that I cannot appeal to my Father, and he will at once send me more than twelve legions of angels? But how then shall the scriptures [*and the Father's will*] be fulfilled? (Matt. 26:52–4)

Mark and Luke then tell us that Jesus turned to the chief priests and officers of the temple and the crowd with them, and reminded them that he had taught openly in the temple and they had not arrested him then, but now they had come with swords and clubs to take him. John has the further memory that Jesus said to those arresting him: 'If it is me you seek, let these [my disciples] go their way.' Mark, however, followed by Matthew, says that all the disciples forsook Jesus and fled.

Mark in his account of the arrest has an intriguing little

paragraph: 'And a young man followed him, with nothing but a linen cloth about his body; and they seized him, but he left the linen cloth and ran away naked' (14:51–2). It is interesting to wonder why Mark should have included a note like this about a seemingly anonymous man. It has been suggested that he was Mark himself, and that Judas had brought the temple police to the upper room hoping to find him there, and not doing so had rushed to Gethsemane where Judas knew that Jesus often went to pray. The parents of Mark thereupon wakened their son and sent him off urgently to warn Jesus and the eleven disciples with him. He had been lurking in the trees, and an attempt was made to seize him. The police had nearly caught him, and he had only eluded arrest by leaving his scanty night attire in their hands.

Jesus is bound and led away to the house of Caiaphas the High Priest, where scribes and elders are already assembled to judge him, the next step in the chain of events we call the passion, the next link, as Christian devotion believes, in the chain of salvation.

9

Three Trials

After his arrest in the garden, Jesus is led away for a Jewish examination before Caiaphas the High Priest. The temple police, the priests, elders and the organised crowd with their prisoner, make their way from Gethsemane up the city side of the Kidron valley, to the house of the High Priest.

Most Christian pilgrims today go to the church of St Peter Galicantu, the church of the cock-crowing, built over the traditional site of the house of Caiaphas. The steps finally leading up to the church are thought by some archaeologists to go back to the time of Jesus, so the pilgrim can feel that here he may be in the footsteps of Jesus, before he enters the church to be hospitably welcomed by the monks in charge of it, who will explain the tradition and show the church's treasures, ancient and modern.

John reports a preliminary questioning before Annas, who had been deposed by the Romans but was still a powerful figure in the Jewish hierarchy, and was also the father-in-law of Caiaphas. Annas was a remarkable man, who had himself been High Priest, and his five sons and son-in-law after him.

Josephus the Jewish historian says that Annas was High Priest AD 7–14. After a short time his son Eleazar held the office for a year. After a year's interval his son-in-law Caiaphas succeeded and was High Priest during the years of Jesus's ministry. After him four more sons became High Priest in turn. Bishop Westcott in his commentary on John's Gospel remarks: 'This mere record reveals the skilful intriguer who exercised through members of his family the headship of his [*priestly*] party.'[1] Annas evidently advised that the accusations against Jesus ought to be heard by his son-in-law, so Jesus was hurried to Caiaphas and the council.

John follows and seems to have some kind of relationship with the High Priest or members of his household and is allowed to enter without question. Peter, who is no coward, as his attempted rescue of Jesus shows, also follows, and is allowed to enter after John has had a word with the portress. It is a cold night and the waiting officers and servants make a fire in the courtyard, and Peter warms himself with others. The maid that kept the door looks suspiciously and closely at him, and then asks, 'Are not you also one of this man's disciples?' The way the question is put suggests that she expects an answer 'yes'. Peter answers shortly, 'I am not!' Some of those warming themselves at the fire now question Peter in the same way, and again he answers, 'I am not.' A little later, a relative of the man whom Peter struck with the sword in the garden asks, 'Did I not see you in the garden with him?' Peter again denies, and others then say that his Galilean accent betrays him.

The explanation of Peter's threefold denial may go back to the warning of Jesus in the upper room, that all the disciples would be offended with him that night, not just frightened or cowardly, but offended with what he was going to do. Matthew reports Peter's words as, 'I know him not', and adds that after the third denial Peter began to curse and swear. It could well be that Peter was hurt at our Lord's rebuke to him in the garden and his refusal of his efforts to rescue him. Peter's words are not just a denial, in fear of being arrested and charged with Jesus. They are a repudiation, as if to mean, 'I am through with him'. As Peter made his angry repudiation the third time, Jesus must have heard him as he was led across the courtyard, for Luke tells us that at that moment 'the Lord turned and looked at Peter'. It must have been a look of sad reproach which went home to Peter's hurt and angry heart. He rushes

---

[1] *The Gospel According to St John, AV, with Introduction and Notes* (London 1892).

away into the darkness and weeps out his penitent heart. He is still the Lord's disciple.

The trial of Jesus proceeds before Caiaphas and the council. Earlier (John 11:48–52) Caiaphas had told his council that the popularity of Jesus was a threatening danger to the Romans, in that he could lead a revolt and proclaim himself king, in which case the Romans would crush it, and they themselves would lose the authority and influence held under Roman suzerainty. 'It is expedient [*therefore*] that one man should die for the people, and that the whole nation should not perish.' John has rather an unexpected comment on this which suggests that the High Priest, by virtue of his office, had the gift of prophecy: 'He did not say this of his own accord but being high priest that year he prophesied that Jesus should die for the nation', though *divinely* meant in a different sense to the one intended. The evangelist then gives his own wider interpretation: 'and not for the nation only, but to gather into one the children of God who are scattered abroad'. Jesus is to be the Gatherer of all who in any way believe in God as the universal Father.

Mark, Matthew and Luke between them tell of mockery in the High Priest's house. Jesus is spat upon, blindfolded, struck, and taunted; 'Prophesy to us, you Christ! Who is it that struck you?' (Mark 14:65; Matt. 26:67–8; Luke 22:63–5).

As soon as it is day the council assembles and endeavours to find a charge that would justify a death sentence. False witnesses are produced but their witness is not consistent. At last two come forward and say that Jesus has threatened to destroy the temple, referring to an incident that is as far back as John 2:18–19, following the cleansing of the temple which John has put at the beginning of the ministry. In that context Jerusalem Jews challenge him to work a miracle which will convince them, to which Jesus replies, 'Destroy this temple and I will raise it up in three days.' John, writing many years after the resurrection, realised that Jesus was referring to the temple of his body.

The evidence offered is so patently false that Jesus does not need to confute it. Matthew tells us that Caiaphas then says, 'I adjure you by the living God, tell us if you are the Christ, the Son of God.' The moment has now come for Jesus to declare himself, and he exclaims, 'You have said so' (meaning those are your words not mine). He continues, 'I tell you, hereafter you will see the Son of man seated at the right hand of Power, and coming on the clouds of heaven', whereupon the High Priest rends his clothes and addresses the council: 'Why do we still need witnesses? You have now heard his blasphemy. What is your judgment?' With one voice they answer, 'He deserves death.' The morning is now come, it is not too early to appeal to the Roman governor. So they bind Jesus and hurry him off to Pontius Pilate (Matt. 26:59–66, 27:1,2).

At this point Matthew (27:1–5) tells us that Judas realises that he has been tricked by the chief priests and elders, and comes back to them to try to rectify the tragic mistake he has made. He brought with him the thirty pieces of silver, which would seem to be convincing evidence that it was not greed for money which was his motive. Most probably the chief priests gave him that sum to give them a hold over him. A considerable number of scholars have thought that Judas wanted to force the hand of Jesus into using the power that all twelve disciples believed he had. Matthew tells us that he pleads with the chief priests, saying, 'I have sinned in betraying innocent blood', to which they reply that this is his responsibility not theirs, whereupon he throws down the thirty pieces of silver into the sanctuary of the temple and rushes out and hangs himself. A recent writer[2] has pointed out that the Greek word used in the gospels to describe the deed of Judas is *paradidomi* which means 'to hand over' and not *prodidomi* meaning 'to betray', so that Judas could better be described as 'the one who handed over Jesus' than 'the one who betrayed Jesus'. If that is so, no ill will, unfaithfulness or secrecy is implied. It could even be that the kiss with which Judas identified Jesus was a genuine

[2] W. H. Vanstone, *The Stature of Waiting* (London 1982).

sign of affection, though we must not forget our Lord's reproach, 'Friend, why are you here?' meaning, 'why are you with these people?' But even the most compassionate reader of this tragic story must agree that what Judas did was a most shameful, wilful and tragic misunderstanding of Jesus, and yet feel that even Judas was included in our Lord's first prayer on the cross, 'Father, forgive them, for they know not what they do.' Peter and Judas both failed their Master: Peter's tears of penitence led to forgiveness; poor Judas could not believe that forgiveness was possible for the awful thing he had done, and as Jesus had warned him he wished he had never been born.

While this sad tragedy is happening, the chief priests and elders take Jesus to the court of Pilate, the Roman governor. Luke tells us, recognising that accusations about a claim to messiahship are not likely to result in a sentence of death, that they add to this basic charge: 'We found this man perverting our nation, and forbidding us to give tribute to Caesar, and saying that he himself is Christ, a king' (23:2–3); both are charges of things he consistently refused to do.

Pilate then asks Jesus, 'Are you the king of the Jews?', to which Jesus replies, 'You have said so', possibly implying that others too are saying this. The result of Pilate's questioning is: 'I find no fault in this man.' The chief priests press further: 'He stirs up the people, teaching throughout all Judaea from Galilee even to this place.' The mention of Galilee suggests a way in which Pilate can avoid making a decision he is reluctant to make. Galilee is under King Herod's jurisdiction, so he sends Jesus to Herod (Luke 23:3–7).

Luke goes on to tell us that Herod was glad of an opportunity to see this man about whom so many people have been talking. Some speak of him as a great wonder-worker and Herod is hopeful that he will work some miracle in his presence. Earlier accounts in the gospel speak of him as possibly conscience-stricken about the execution of John the Baptist, and having a superstitious fear that Jesus is the Baptist returning to haunt him. He puts question after question to Jesus, but Jesus refuses to answer, maintaining a dignity of silence in the face of Herod's curiosity and unserious attitude.

Herod and his soldiers then proceed to mock Jesus and, as Mark and Matthew report was done in Pilate's court a little later, an old purple cloak is thrown around his shoulders in a parody of royalty. Jesus is then sent back to Pilate, with no verdict which will relieve Pilate of the responsibility of decision. Herod, however, is grateful to Pilate for the courtesy of being consulted, and a coolness which had arisen between them is set right (Luke 23:8–12).

John (18:28–40) has quite a lengthy account of Pilate's examination of Jesus and of his reluctance to be pressurised into passing the sentence which the chief priests want. They refuse to enter the judgment hall lest they should become defiled by so doing and be debarred from eating the Passover. (John clearly differs from the other three evangelists, to him the Passover has not yet been celebrated; they agree that it had been eaten the night before.) So Pilate and Jesus confront one another without their presence. Pilate again asks his prisoner, 'Are you the king of the Jews?'

Jesus answers, 'My kingship is not of this world.' If it were, his servants would be fighting to protect him. 'My kingship is very different.' Pilate is quick to see an implied admission: 'So you are a king, then?' Jesus goes on to explain that his kingdom is a kingdom of truth, and that he was born to bear witness to this truth, and all who make a stand for truth will recognise this. Pilate replies, 'What is truth?' This need not be the cynical answer that is the opening sentence of Bacon's essay on truth: ' "What is truth?" asked jesting Pilate, and did not wait for an answer.' It is a question to which every just judge wants an answer, and Pilate was trying to be just. The difficulty of finding out the truth from witnesses who differ diametrically, or from prosecuting or defending counsel's conjectures of what happened, is a real one. To John the whole life of Jesus said 'I am the truth'. Pilate was evidently impressed, for he goes out again to the waiting priests and tells them: 'I find no crime in him.'

He then thinks of a way which might enable him to release Jesus. As a goodwill gesture there is an agreed custom that the Governor should release a prisoner at the time of the Passover. Pilate offers to release Jesus whom he calls 'the king of the Jews', to which the rulers and the crowd shout: 'Not this man, but Barabbas!' It would appear that there had already been agreement to ask for Barabbas, who was in prison charged with robbery, sedition and murder (Luke 23:19). The shouts prevail. Pilate's latest effort to release Jesus fails.

Pilate then orders Jesus to be scourged. This is done and while waiting in the guard room the soldiers mock him; plaiting a crown of thorns they put it on his head, and array him in a purple robe, possibly the same old one thrown over his shoulders by Herod's men, and jeering, 'Hail, King of the Jews'.

Pilate, hoping the scourging will satisfy the crowd, sends Jesus out again and repeats, 'I find no crime in him.' So Jesus comes out wearing the crown of thorns and the purple robe. Pilate says to them, 'Here is the man.'

(The portrayal of this moment in the ITV 'Jesus of Nazareth' was for many the most moving moment in the whole feature, and many of those who watched could not hold back their tears.)

But the inflamed crowd shout again and again, 'Crucify him! Crucify him!'

To this frenzied shout Pilate replies, 'Take him yourselves and crucify him, for I find no crime in him.' They reply that by their law Jesus ought to die, because he has made himself out to be the Son of God. Somehow this argument seems to shake the Governor. There is a mystery about Jesus which Pilate cannot fathom. He enters the praetorium again to question Jesus further. Jesus is silent, whereupon Pilate warns him that he has power to release him or crucify him. This moves Jesus to say, 'You would have no power over me unless it had been given you from above', perhaps meaning that all that is allowed to happen lies within the purpose of God, implying his unshaken faith in the Father.

Pilate still wants to release Jesus but the chief priests now bring forward what seems to them a conclusive answer: 'If you release this man you are not Caesar's friend', meaning that Pilate is no longer a loyal representative of the emperor, with the implied threat that they will report the matter to Rome. Pilate cannot resist a last taunt to the accusers, 'Shall I crucify your king?' He must have given a cynical smile as they reply, 'We have no king but Caesar!' (John 19:1–16).

He hands Jesus over to be crucified.

10

On the Way to the Cross

After the Governor's reluctant sentence of death Jesus is led away into the palace until arrangements for his execution are made. Mark tells us that the whole battalion of troops is called together, though he does not tell us what number that would involve. Pilate is leaving nothing to chance; lest there should be further riot or lest there should be an attempt at rescue or even lest the accusation of the Jewish authorities should be true that Jesus is setting himself up as king.

So Jesus wearing the crown of thorns and the worn out purple cloak, with his back still bleeding from the scourging, is now at the mercy of a large number of soldiers, as he had been when appearing before Herod. They strike him, spit upon him, kneel before him in mock homage, shouting in derision, 'Hail, King of the Jews!' As the hour of 9 a.m. comes near they take off the purple cloak, 'put on him his own clothes' (presumably those that had been removed for the scourging), and lead him out to be crucified (Mark 15:16–20). Christian disciples in every generation, following in dismayed imagination this succession of insults, humiliations, rejections and physical cruelty, at each passiontide, realise more deeply what it cost him in attempting to prove that there is no limit to God's love and forgiveness.

John supplies the next link in the way of the cross: 'They took Jesus, and he went out, bearing his own cross, to the place called the place of a skull, which is called Golgotha' (19:17). By this time Jesus must have been exhausted, stumbling and falling under the weight of the cross. The other three evangelists tell us that the escorting soldiers and Jerusalem leaders then notice a man coming into the city from the country-side. Later they learn that he is a man from Africa, Simon of Cyrene. Mark adds that he was the father of Alexander and Rufus who would probably be known to the Christians in Rome for whom Mark wrote his Gospel, which later tradition says was based on the reminiscences of his uncle Peter, for whom he acted as interpreter. It would therefore be reasonable to suppose that Simon became a disciple and his two sons with him. So Simon carried the cross for the rest of the way. We can be sure that Jesus was grateful, and equally certain that many generations of Christians have felt grateful to this man from Africa. There was an even greater load on the heart of Jesus, which only he could carry: the burden of rejection and fanatical intolerance of his own people; and the greatest burden of the sins of all mankind in every age, which alienate them from God.

Every Friday groups of monks and pilgrims follow the stations of the cross and on Good Friday there are many such groups. At each station they stand in silence and then pray a short litany together. It is not a long journey, and it has to be made through people, some on donkeys and others pushing carts full of fruit and vegetables, loaves of bread or carcasses of meat for the shoppers in the bazaars that line both sides of the narrow streets.

Recently the Mayor and Municipality of Jerusalem have been renewing the sewers, buried electric cables and pavements of the city. In the course of their excavations the workmen have unearthed some paving stones which archaeologists think go back to the time of Jesus. So Christians can reverently hope that they are treading in the last footsteps of Jesus.

Luke adds another incident on the Via Dolorosa, namely the meeting with some of the compassionate women of Jerusalem, who followed the great crowd of people. It is surmised that some of these made a charitable practice of refreshing the criminals as they were hurried to the place of execution. The legend of Veronica who wiped the bloodstained face of Jesus may go back to this incident. Luke tells us that they and the crowd 'lamented and bewailed him'. Jesus stops for a moment and turns to them, saying, 'Daughters of Jerusalem, do not weep for me, but weep for yourselves and your children.' This is his final lament over Jerusalem (Luke 23:27–31).

Luke's Gospel (13:31–5) tells us of two earlier occasions when Jesus had grieved over Jerusalem. The first was in Galilee when he had begun what was to be his last journey to Jerusalem. As he journeyed through towns and villages some friendly Pharisees warned him that Herod wanted to kill him. Jesus replied that he must finish his course, and then he must expect the death which Jerusalem meets out to its prophets, and which he is ready to accept. He goes on in words which reveal both his grief over Jerusalem and the tenderness of his love for it: 'O Jerusalem, Jerusalem, killing the prophets and stoning them who are sent to you. How often would I have gathered your children together, as a hen gathers her brood under her wings, and you would not.' He sees quite clearly the inevitable consequences of their rejection. Yet there is an ultimate hope that one day they will see him and recognise him in words which are reserved for the Messiah: 'Blessed is he who comes in the name of the Lord.'

The second of these occasions is when the procession from Bethany to Jerusalem, on what we Christians call Palm Sunday, comes in sight of the city, with its walls and the temple as restored by Herod the Great, when Jesus bursts into tears, because it is missing its greatest moment, and fails to recognise 'the things that belong unto peace'. We have already meditated on this incident in Chapter 5, but we can never plumb the depths of our Lord's love and grief over Jerusalem, but can only murmur with him, 'O Jerusalem, Jerusalem!' (Luke 19:41–4).

Perhaps by the time Luke put his Gospel together Jerusalem had been destroyed, the temple had been desecrated, the last desperate stand had been made at Massada, ending in the beseiged committing suicide together. It is moving to note that it was the one Gentile writer in the New Testament who had gathered the memories of eyewitnesses, had himself seen the fulfilment of our Lord's forebodings, who entered so deeply into his love of Jerusalem and grief over it. Luke's Gospel and the first history of the early Church and its expansion into the Roman world had the aim of showing to Theophilus that Rome need not fear and persecute the Christian Church and that its people might share in the good news brought by Jesus from God and the blessings consequent on his life, teaching, death and spiritual presence. Luke had had the advantage of being a close friend of Paul and seeing the amazing change that had come into his life, which had given him the vision of a world for God that Jesus had.

It is moving to ponder over Christians' love of Jerusalem down the ages, how even today a pilgrimage to it is for almost all the journey of a lifetime, despite the transfer of Christian vision and devotion to the heavenly Jerusalem, the perfected and eternal city which is to be the mother of all seekers of God and his truth. Even among the crusaders with their mistaken view that holy places are more important to God than people, and even allowing that the behaviour of many crusaders fell woefully short of Christ-like imitation, there was a love and reverence for the earthly Jerusalem. The visit of Helena, the mother of the first Roman emperor to become a disciple, with her desire to identify the significant sites in the life of Jesus, is further evidence of Christian love for the earthly Jerusalem.

Muhammad in his early years as a prophet directed his followers to face Jerusalem at their five times of daily prayer. In the earliest mosques the 'Qibla' showed Muslim worshippers the direction of Jerusalem, and it was only after the rejection of his prophethood by Jews and Christians alike that the direction of the 'Qibla' was changed towards Mecca. His mystical journey to heaven began at Jerusalem. After the capture of Jerusalem, Muslims built the lovely mosque of Omar over the rock on which Abraham was willing to offer his much-loved son.

Our Jewish half-brothers and sisters during the centuries of dispersion and exile maintained hope and faith in their ultimate return in the mutual salutation, 'Next year in Jerusalem', which today is being adopted by Palestinians.

Nor can we forget the gesture of General Allenby when he entered Jerusalem to receive the surrender of the Turks during the First World War, in dismounting from his horse to enter the city so much associated with the author of his own faith. Many pilgrims to Jerusalem today will be reminded of another soldier's devotion in General Gordon's search for the 'place of the skull' and his numinous feeling that the garden tomb was the original site. Whether that is historically identified no one can say with certainty. What we can be sure of is that the original tomb must have been very like it. And there is the text in John's Gospel (19:41), 'Now in the place where he was crucified there was a garden'. The peace and beauty of today's garden commemorates the fact of the resurrection, rather than its geographical detail.

We have lingered a long time at this spiritual station of the cross, with our gratitude to the women of Jerusalem who wept over Jesus as he passed on his way to Calvary. We in imaginative devotion move with him.

11

Responsibility for the Cross

Arrived at Golgotha, the place shaped like a skull, outside the city walls Jesus is stripped of his clothes, stretched out on the cross, his hands and feet are nailed and the cross is raised into its socket, a moment of excruciating agony impossible to imagine in all its pain.

At that moment all that bursts from his lips is another great prayer of the passion: 'Father, forgive them for they know not what they do' (Luke 23:34), a prayer for all who had any responsibility in bringing him there. Not only does Jesus pray for forgiveness but he makes excuse for all involved, implying that if they only knew what they were doing, if they only knew the love and forgiveness in the heart of the one nailed there, they would not have done it.

Included in it would be the soldiers who did the actual nailing, a squad of four under a centurion, though the whole garrison would be on alert for any trouble. The men on duty were probably hardened by many crucifixions of criminals and rebels. The clothes of the men crucified were their perquisites. In this case having divided the garments of Jesus, they were left with the outer tunic which could not be divided without making it useless. So they threw dice at the foot of the cross to decide who should have it. 'Father, forgive *them*.'

All down the centuries most Christians have held the Jewish people for ever guilty of deicide, the killing of one whom we regard as the only true Son of God. The result has been ostracism, persecution or acquiescence in persecution of the Jewish people, and the accusation that this treatment prepared a prejudicing atmosphere which Hitler and the Nazis exploited in the Holocaust, its gas chambers and the mass murder of six million Jews.

Jesus had his friends, the man from whom he borrowed the donkey and its foal, the man who at an agreed time could be recognised as bearing a pitcher of water on his head, to whom Peter and John were to say, 'The master says, "Where is the guest chamber for the Passover meal?" ' There were the Galilean pilgrims who accompanied him into Jerusalem, who, strangers in the city, would be innocently sleeping in their beds while the chief priests organised the crowd outside the Governor's palace demanding the death penalty. We have already mentioned the weeping women of Jerusalem and the sorrowing crowd that followed the cross. Finally Luke tells us that when the execution was over 'all the multitudes who assembled to see the sight, when they saw what had taken place, returned home beating their breasts' (23:48). Following Luke it could well be that there were more people in Jerusalem that evening who regretted what had happened than those who approved it.

A prayer of the saintly Pope John XXIII, clearly inspired by the first prayer from the cross, can well sum up our meditation on the involvement of some Jews and the wholesale condemnation of all Jews by many Christians:

O God, we are conscious that many centuries of blindness have blinded our eyes so that we no longer see the beauty of thy chosen people, nor recognise in their faces and features our privileged brethren. We realise that the mark of Cain stands upon our foreheads. Across the centuries our brother Abel has lain in the blood which we drew or which we caused to be shed by forgetting thy love. Forgive us for the curse we falsely attached to their name as Jews. Forgive us for crucifying thee a second time in their flesh. For we knew not what we did.

A heavy responsibility rests on Pilate, the Roman Governor, who in spite of repeated declarations that he found no crime in Jesus, yet, pressurised by the Jewish authorities and an organised crowd, finally condemned him to death. His action reported by Matthew cannot excuse him, any more than the fanatical cry of the crowd can implicate later generations of Jews:

> So when Pilate saw that he was gaining nothing, but rather that a riot was beginning, he took water and washed his hands before the crowd, saying, 'I am innocent of this man's blood; see to it yourselves.' And all the people answered, 'His blood be on us and on our children!' Then he released Barabbas for them, and having scourged Jesus, delivered him to be crucified. (Matt. 27:24–6)

Jesus, as reported by John, understood Pilate's dilemma: 'He who delivered me to you has the greater sin' (19:11). There was a sin in Pilate, but an even greater sin in the religious authorities who brought Jesus before him.

We have already considered the part played by Judas and the possibility that he wanted to put Jesus into a position where he would use the power that he believed Jesus possessed. Judas was the only southerner in the twelve chosen disciples, and during the two or three years of the ministry Jesus must have come to know him well, and to be aware of his mistaken ideas of messiahship. Jesus must have prayed about Judas in the night he spent in prayer before choosing the twelve (Luke 6:12–14). There must have been something about him, he acted as treasurer of the small money resources of the band, and it would be easy for later writers to accuse him of dishonesty after he had handed Jesus over to the temple authorities. Knowing Jesus through study of the gospels and through years of his fulfilling promise of spiritual presence with us, and prayer to him and through him, we can be sure that Judas was in his prayer from the cross, and in the conclusion that he like all others involved in the chain of responsibility did not fully realise what he was doing. When he did, poor Judas was full of remorse, but remorse is despair. Judas could not believe that there was any possibility of forgiveness for what he had done.

It might be thought that some responsibility rested on the other eleven disciples. Mark and Matthew both say that after the arrest of Jesus in Gethsemane they all forsook him and fled. Had they all remained with Jesus and been arrested with him, Pilate might have hesitated to sentence all to be crucified. John, however, reports Jesus as saying to his captors, 'If you seek me, let these men go', and adds that this was a fulfilment of our Lord's words in the great prayer (John 17), 'of those whom thou gavest me, I lost not one' (18:8-9). The reader may feel that he does not have to choose between these two accounts. Jesus may have had in mind that, if all the disciples perished with him, there would be no one left to witness to the good news he brought from God and the saving love which he was determined to show in the last hours of his incarnate life, and his full confidence that God would act in answer to his trusting acceptance of the divine will. Thereupon the eleven, who had not been named or identified, quietly withdrew into the darkness of the garden. Three days later ten of them were together in the upper room, when the faith of Jesus in the Father's will was vindicated, and the doors barred in fear could not keep the risen Lord out.

Had there been no human sin and at every stage of development humans had lived in dependence upon God and in obedience to him the cross might never have been necessary. What we speak of as the 'Fall' happened in the earliest humans and certainly happens in every one of us. One of the prayers in the ancient late night service of compline bids us pray, 'Make us so to abound in sorrow for our sins which were the cause of thy passion.' So the sinfulness of humanity cries out for forgiveness and reconciliation. It has been said that there was a cross in the heart of God before there was ever one on Calvary, expressing in human symbolism and words the divine grief over human sin. Jesus in talking with Peter about the need for his followers to forgive one another the sins against them, had underlined this, when he answered Peter's question about repeated forgiveness, 'not seven times, but seventy times seven', meaning unlimited forgivingness. Jesus on the cross showed that there was nothing which we could do to him and to God, which God would not forgive.

I remember hearing a story in a Three Hours service which I attended as a choirboy, of a man who had committed almost every kind of sin. When the awful succession of sins came home to him he went to the parish priest, and having confessed the many he remembered asked if forgiveness could possibly be available for such a sinner as he now knew himself to have been. The priest replied, 'My son, I have never heard such a dreadful list of sins. You must go to the bishop and put your question to him.' So he went to the bishop who urged him to take his question to the Holy Father in Rome. There he poured out his heart to the Pope, who replied, 'My son, my son, I dare not give you the answer you hope for, sooner would this staff I hold in my hand burst into flower, like Aaron's rod.' Sadly the man left the chapel and slowly made his way down the corridor leading to St. Peter's Square. He had not gone very far when he heard an excited voice calling, 'Come back, come back! The Holy Father bids you come back.' He retraced his steps to the chapel he had left a minute before, and as he entered he saw that the staff in the Holy Father's hand had burst into flower.

That is only a story, and the critical mind can pick many holes in it, but the memory of it can still move to tears one who heard it over seventy years ago. The critics said to Jesus, 'Only God can forgive sins', when he said to the paralytic in Capernaum, 'Son, your sins are forgiven you.' On the first Easter evening the risen Master sent his apostles out to the world. They now had a gospel of love and forgiveness to tell people, and a promise that acting on his behalf and with his authority they could forgive sins (John 20:23).

Christians have sometimes thought of God as a stern and righteous God who demanded a perfect sacrifice before he would forgive and save, contrasting the merciful Jesus with the stern divine Judge. Such a contrast is contrary to the teaching of the New Testament: 'God was in Christ reconciling the world to himself, not counting their trespasses against them, and entrusting to us the message of reconciliation' (2 Cor. 5:19).

At other times Christians have thought of Christ as paying a ransom for men. Jesus himself said that he had come to give his life as a ransom for all. The question arises as to whom the ransom was paid. It could not possibly be to the devil. A loving God who always takes the initiative would not require a ransom. What that text expresses is the cost of proving to men the infinite love and the limitless forgiveness of God. Jesus had said to his disciples, 'Greater love has no man than this, that a man lay down his life for his friends' (John 15:13). Jesus did more than this, as Paul points out:

> While we were still weak, at the right time Christ died for the ungodly. Why, one will hardly die for a righteous man – though perhaps for a good man one will dare even to die. But God shows his love for us in that while we were yet sinners Christ died for us. Since, therefore, we are now justified by his blood, much more shall we be saved by him from the wrath of God. (Rom. 5:6–9)

There are some awful sins today which individuals, groups and nations find difficult to forgive. The eternal Christ includes them all in that first prayer from the cross – terrorists, drop-outs, muggers, oppressing governments, war-mongers, surrogate murderers, rapists, as well as the killer sins of hatred, pride and greed, self-seeking and hypocrisy. Those of us who emphasise being respectable may find that we are more troubled by what I have called the 'killer sins'. My own personal faith is that God forgives before we repent, and that it is his forgiveness that moves us to repent. The releasing, saving words said by Jesus as he looked in compassion on the Capernaum paralytic let down through the roof at his feet were, 'Son, your sins are forgiven.' He said the same thing to the woman of the city, who was a sinner, who intruded into the Pharisee's house to anoint the feet of Jesus with ointment and tears, 'Your sins are forgiven', and from that moment she was the woman who had once been a sinner (Luke 7:48).

In the Authorised Version of the Bible, there is a similar incident printed in John 7:53–8:11, which some ancient manuscripts put after Luke 21:38, an incident which most readers feel is true to the spirit of Jesus, whatever the textual context. A woman caught in the act of adultery is brought before Jesus by the scribes and Pharisees, who quote the law of Moses that she should be stoned. Jesus says to the man who had brought her to him, 'He that is without sin among you, let him first cast a stone at her', and waits in silence for their reaction. One or two of the older men, conscious possibly of more sins than the younger, go away and are followed by the others, until Jesus and the woman only are left. He asks her, 'Hath no man condemned thee?' to which she answers, 'No man, Lord.' The Lord replies, 'Neither do I condemn thee: go and sin no more.'

Forgiveness can only become effective when accepted, and that means that the sinner feels in a different way and hates his sin and longs for amending grace. All sinners are commanded by the forgiving Lord to 'go and sin no more'.

The writer of the Epistle to the Hebrews has a very stern warning:

> For it is impossible to restore again to repentence those who have once been enlightened, who have tasted the heavenly gift, and have become partakers of the Holy Spirit, and have tasted the goodness of the word of God and the powers of the age to come, if they then commit apostasy, since they crucify the Son of God on their own account and hold him up to contempt. (Heb. 6:4–6)

The student of the gospels must surely believe and hope that the writer of Hebrews is mistaken, but can readily accept the thought that those who continue in sin or fall away after the assurance of forgiveness are guilty of crucifying the Son of God afresh.

This long meditation may appropriately end with writer and

reader gratefully and penitently making John Donne's prayer
and poem their own.

> Wilt Thou forgive that sin where I begun,
>   Which was my sin, though it were done before?
> Wilt Thou forgive that sin, through which I run,
>   And do run still, though still I do deplore?
>   When Thou hast done, Thou hast not done,
>   For I have more.
>
> Wilt Thou forgive that sin which I have won
>   Others to sin, and made my sin their door?
> Wilt Thou forgive that sin which I did shun
>   A year, or two: but wallowed in, a score?
>   When Thou hast done, Thou hast not done,
>   For I have more.
>
> I have a sin of fear, that when I have spun
>   My last thread, I shall perish on the shore;
> But swear by Thy self, that at my death Thy Son
>   Shall shine as he shines now, and heretofore;
>   And, having done that, Thou hast done;
>   I fear no more.
>
>   ('A Hymn to God the Father')

12

The Powerlessness of the Cross

Many of those standing near the cross were supporters of the rulers and chief priests who had plotted the death of Jesus. Mark and Matthew note their satisfaction that he was now on the cross:

> And those that passed by derided him, wagging their heads, and saying, 'Aha! You who would destroy the temple and build it in three days, save yourself and come down from the cross!' So also the chief priests mocked him to one another with the scribes, saying, 'He saved others; he cannot save himself. Let the Christ, the king of Israel, come down from the cross, that we may see and believe.' (Mark 15:29–32)

Most of what was shouted to him was mockery and insult, but one jeer was an unintended tribute, 'He saved others; he cannot save himself.' We who know Jesus from the gospels and from our discipleship, cannot think of a greater tribute.

Catherine of Sienna (1333–80), a member of the Third Order of St Dominic, who gave herself to contemplation and the care of the poor, and did much to heal the Great Schism in the papacy, and wrote many spiritual letters, said, 'Nails were not enough to hold God-and-Man nailed and fastened to the Cross, had love not held him there.'[1] Certainly it was love that brought him to the cross, and that love continued through the hours on the cross, but in his full humanity he was powerless to come

[1] Quoted by Eric Milner-White, in *A Procession of Passion Prayers* (London 1950).

down. Paul says of Jesus, 'though he was in the form of God
. . . emptied himself, taking the form of a servant, being born
in the likeness of men. And being found in human form he
humbled himself and became obedient unto death, even death
on a cross' (Phil. 2:6–8). Nails indeed held him there, he could
not come down, as hundreds of others crucified and martyred
could not come down. Paul bids his friends at Philippi and all
who in any age read his letter, 'Have this mind among yourselves, which is yours in Christ Jesus' (2:5).

All down the ages since humans became consciously thinking
and feeling beings, many have thought that the most character-
istic attribute of God is power. The apostle John who knew
Jesus more intimately than any of the others who had been
with him throughout the ministry, and who often spoke of
himself as 'the disciple whom Jesus loved', tells us that love is
the very essence of God. 'God is love and those who abide in
love abide in God and God abides in them.' John goes on to
say, 'We love because he first loved us' (1 John 4:16, 19). Jesus
on the cross was undefeatedly loving; humanly speaking he was
powerless. It has been said, 'It is strange that Jesus should
claim to reveal God best of all, not by his works of power but
by his weakness, not by what he did but by what he suffered.'

William Temple during the years of the Second World War
wrestled with the relationship of love and power. He spoke of
the kingdom of God as absolute power controlled by perfect
love, an insight which could inspire and guide all in positions
of responsibility and political power.[2]

I believe that we must take this insight of power and powerlessness back into our thinking about God as Creator. He has
handed over responsibility to humans, as the writer of the first
chapter of Genesis believed: 'And God blessed them, and God
said to them, "Be fruitful and multiply and fill the earth and
subdue it" ' (Gen. 1:28).

One of the psalmists also speaks of this delegated authority
and consequent responsibility: 'All the whole heavens are the

[2] *Readings in St John's Gospel*, 2 vols. (London 1939, 1940).

71

Lord's: the earth has he given to the children of men' (Ps. 115:16).

Michael Ramsey, in a sermon preached in Australia, speaks of the relationship of desire for power and fear: 'The human race is afraid and its fears are about power – about having it or not having it. Those who have it are frightened that they may be going to lose it. Those who do not have it are frightened of those with it. This is true of groups, classes, nations and races.'

The apostle John again comes to our rescue: 'There is no fear in love, but perfect love casts out fear. For fear has to do with punishment, and he who fears is not perfected in love' (1 John 4:18). Who could be afraid of a baby lying in a manger for a cradle in the stable of the Bethlehem caravanserai? Who could be afraid of a man powerless on a cross? The defenceless-ness of Bethlehem and the powerlessness of Calvary are indica-tive of God putting himself into the hands of men. Both speak to us of the divine recognition of how far God-in-Christ is prepared to go to deal with our ignorance of him, and our alienation and estrangement from him. 'God was in Christ reconciling the world to himself, not counting their trespasses against them, and entrusting to us the message of reconciliation' (2 Cor. 5:19). Christ is ambassador and representative, always taking the initiative, but always consulting the One who sent him.

We have thought before in our meditations that God's will for Jesus was to be unfailing in love, even on the cross, more than ever on the cross. He would not force men, he would win them by love. He wanted them to love God freely, by their own choice and decision. He had accepted an interpretation of the Messiah that only a few prophetic souls had seen – a suffering Messiah, at the mercy of rejection, pain and death. The New Testament insists that in this Jesus is so amazingly like God, and that God is so wonderfully like Jesus. If God is like the human video shown us in Jesus, then our minds and hearts can be at peace and joyfully so.

We humans are always expecting Jesus to come down from

the cross and clear up the mess that we make of the world. We blasphemously think that God is responsible for everything that happens. We expect him to work miracles in conditions that we have created, and which can only be set right if we live in his way.

God does work miracles but they are not external miracles, but miracles within the spirit of man. The miracle that I ought to expect and pray for is: 'Create and make in me a new and contrite heart, O God, and renew a right spirit within me.' The Spirit of God will suggest to us holy desires, inspired initiations and good plans, and just actions and behaviour, and will strengthen our spirits to practise these consistently, and to go on faithfully, whether we feel like it or not, come whatever wind or weather.

Paul tells us how he personally has experienced the effectiveness of powerlessness. Evidently he suffered from some disablement or chronic complaint, which he speaks of as a thorn in the flesh and a harassment of Satan, in this way recognising that it was not caused by God's will. He goes on, 'Three times I besought the Lord about this, that it should leave me; but he said to me, "My grace is sufficient for you, for my power is made perfect in weakness . . . for when I am weak, then I am strong" ' (2 Cor. 12:7–10). God's grace gets its opportunity when we are so weak, so much at our wit's end that we have to throw ourselves upon him, an ideal situation to be in, easy enough to talk about or quote to others, but difficult to remember and practise ourselves. That trust in supporting grace is indeed a miracle.

The early Church had very little in the way of wealth or influence:

For consider your call, brethren; not many of you were wise according to worldly standards, not many were powerful, not many were of noble birth; but God chose what is foolish in the world to shame the wise, God chose what is weak in the world to shame the strong, God chose what is low and despised in the world, even things that are not, to bring to nothing things that are, so that no human being might boast in the presence of God. (1 Cor. 1:26–30)

Yet that body of somewhat insignificant people was able to withstand local harassment and imperial persecution, until at length it became an allowed institution, the emperor became a Christian and his mother made a pilgrimage to try and identify the holy places.

The Church is very different now: we number at least a thousand million adherents, one quarter of the population of the world. We can influence governments. We own extremely valuable property making us possibly the most wealthy corporation in the world.

We have ranged far in time, geography and meditation. Let us return to our starting point, Christ hanging powerlessly on his cross, flanked by two thieves. Let a Christian poet call us back, not for a quick reading, but thoughtfully letting each line take us deeper into the mystery and the wonder:

If we have never sought, we seek Thee now:
Thine eyes burn through the dark, our only stars:
We must have sight of thorn-pricks on thy brow,
We must have Thee, O Jesus of the scars.

The heavens frighten us: they are too calm,
In all the Universe we have no place.
Our wounds are hurting us, where is the balm?
O Jesus, by thy scars we claim thy grace.

If when the doors are shut, Thou drawest near,
Only reveal those hands, that side of Thine:
We know today what wounds are, we have no fear.
Show us thy scars, we know the countersign.

The other gods were strong; but Thou wast weak;

They rode, but Thou didst stumble to a throne;
But to our wounds only God's wounds can speak.
And not a God has wounds but THOU ALONE.[3]

[3] From Edward Shillito, *Jesus of the Scars and Other Poems*; quoted by William Temple in *Readings in St John's Gospel*.

13

The Pain of the Cross

Crucifixion is a barbarous and cruel way of death. Jesus hung on the cross for six hours, from nine o'clock to three o'clock.

The chief thing that the ITV 'Jesus of Nazareth' brought home to me was the awful physical pain, the dragging weight on the arms, the impossibility of changing position to make the pain more bearable.

Yet the only words referring to the physical pain were, 'I thirst'. Jesus was now experiencing what he had spoken of to Peter, when refusing his courageous one-man attempt at rescue in the garden of Gethsemane: 'Shall I not drink the cup which the Father has given me?' (John 18:11) His unwavering conviction at every step was that this was the Father's will and would manifest the divine love and forgiveness. The writer of the Letter to Hebrew Christians confirms this:

> When Christ came into the world, he said, 'Sacrifices and offerings thou hast not desired, but a body hast thou prepared for me; in burnt offerings and sin offerings thou hast taken no pleasure.' Then I said, 'Lo, I have come to do thy will, O God,' as it is written of me in the roll of the book. (Heb. 10:5–7)

When the soldiers heard the dry-throated cry of Jesus, 'I thirst', one of them, possibly the centurion who was to pay him a tribute after he had died, soaked a sponge in the rough wine they had brought with them to refresh themselves during the growing heat of the day, put it on a javelin or spear and lifted it to his mouth, a kindly deed for which Christians, meditating on the cross, are forever grateful. (John 19:28–9)

Mark, followed by Matthew and Luke, tells us that there was darkness over the whole land from the sixth to the ninth hour. Possibly the khamsin, the hot wind from the desert, was blowing, laden with yellow sand, obscuring the sun, and creating an eerie feeling in all who were watching. (This actually happened on one of the days of my first Holy Week in Jerusalem.) Towards the end of this period, Mark and Matthew tell us that Jesus cried out with a loud voice, 'Eloi, Eloi, lama sabacthani?', which means 'My God, My God, why hast Thou forsaken me?' (Mark 15:34, Matt. 27:46). During over sixty years of attending devotional services on Good Friday I have heard preachers, and have indeed myself preached, on the darkness in the soul of Jesus, of his loneliness on the cross when even God seemed hidden. Such an interpretation now seems to focus attention on the second half of the cry expressing pain and desolation and not enough on the magnificent faith of the repeated 'My God'. Certainly we can imagine that the spirit of evil, who tried to deflect his faith and obedience in the forty days retreat in the wilderness after his baptism, would have been aware that the last and fiercest strife had arrived and had insinuated a final temptation, 'What if God has also forsaken you?'

The words uttered by Jesus in this 'darkness over all the land' were the first verse from one of the great psalms of the Hebrew Bible, Psalm 22. It is quite possible that Jesus went through the whole of this psalm in meditation, just as those conducting services today often announce the number of the psalm chosen, and add the words of the first verse, and then minister and people together recite the whole psalm.

Psalm 22 is a cry of perplexity and pain of one who at its beginning feels that he is abandoned by God, yet he still calls out, 'My God! *My* God!' However much he fears and feels that God has forsaken him, he does not forsake God. In the first twenty-two verses he pours out his heart to God in despair; the remaining verses are a hymn of praise and thanksgiving, showing that his prayer has been answered. So the whole psalm is a moving expression of faith.

In the opening verses he describes his despair and the mocking of his enemies. He feels that he is like a worm, trodden underfoot, not treated as a human being. His long continued loneliness and suffering make others feel that his former professions of faith cannot have been sincere, otherwise God would have rescued him by this time. Yet in the depths he remembers how God delivered the fathers in Israel, and he still hangs on to his belief that God is holy and righteous. This section ends with the taunt, 'He trusted in God, that he would deliver him: let him deliver him, if he will have him.'

These mocking words only remind him of God's care since his birth, but now he compares his enemies with wild bulls and lions that roar and rend. He appeals to God, 'O go not from me', for there is no one else to help him.

He goes on to describe his physical suffering, fevered and emaciated, his limbs hardly function, his bones stick out, and worst of all his heart is like melting wax, all courage and strength gone. Again he prays, 'O Lord, do not stand far off: You are my helper, hasten to my aid' (v. 19).

In the second half of the psalm (vv. 23–32) there is a marked change of mood. The psalmist's prayer has been answered. His heart is full of gratitude and his voice bursts into praise. He wants all his friends to know what God has done for him, and the whole congregation of Israel to hear his grateful thanksgiving. He invites the poor and humble to share in his sacrifice and blesses his guests, 'May your hearts rejoice for ever' (v. 26).

His thought and vision spread out further to all the nations, 'Let all the ends of the earth remember and turn to the Lord . . . for the kingdom is the Lord's: and he shall be ruler over the nations' (vv. 28–9).

His faith has not yet extended to those who have died, yet perhaps in verse 30 there is a note of regret and a hint of hope.

He concludes with the assurance that his children will know

of God's blessing to him: 'a future generation as yet unborn shall learn of the Lord's goodness' (vv. 30–1).

I think of Jesus hanging on the cross in all that pain, yet with the faith that the farthest ends of the earth will turn to God as a result, and all nations shall come to worship him. The Christian can only stand in awe and admiration before such faith and hear the whisper in the heart, 'This is indeed the Saviour of the world, and my Saviour.'

All four gospels speak of Jesus warning both his disciples and hearers that they too must expect to be cross-bearers:

> And he called to him the multitude with his disciples, and said to them, 'If any man would come after me, let him deny himself and take up his cross and follow me. For whoever would save his life will lose it; and whoever loses his life for my sake and the gospel's will save it. For what does it profit a man, to gain the whole world and forfeit his life? For what can a man give in return for his life? For whoever is ashamed of me and of my words in this adulterous and sinful generation, of him will the Son of man also be ashamed, when he comes in the glory of his Father with the holy angels.' (Mark 8:34–8)

The test of whether I am a true disciple or not is whether I repudiate self-interest as the chief motive of my life; whether I accept what life or other people lay upon me. There must be on my spiritual shoulder the bruise of the cross I have to carry. To many it may look as if I hate my life. Jesus by using words which may seem an exaggeration, drives home to me his demand for full discipleship. Luke records Jesus as applying his teaching to personal relationships: 'If anyone comes to me and does not hate his own father and mother and wife and children and brothers and sisters, yea and even his own life, he cannot be my disciple' (14:26). This is taking the first great commandment of God's law, to love God with all my heart, mind, life and will, into the area of the second command to love my neighbour. Putting God first does not mean that I love others less, but that all lesser loves are loved in God's way, as he and his first and perfect Son love.

That first Good Friday there were three men carrying to the place of execution the cross on which each was to be crucified. There was Jesus himself, stumbling under his cross, there was the robber whom we speak of as the penitent thief, who realised that his own actions had brought him there, and the poor hardened thief who cursed against everything and everybody.

A misgiving will come into the soul of many of us: what if I have been partly or wholly responsible for my own cross, by wrong attitudes, ignorance and weakness? When I realise this, I become penitent, I regret the past, I want to set it right, I want to be forgiven and helped to a new life. I am liberated from the past. I accept God's forgiveness and his promise of grace to bear the consequences of my sin and enable me to live as God's child and Christ's disciple.

Faith is called for – to believe that our lesser crosses, purged from past responsibility, can lead to new life, to liberation from the load of guilt, to reconciliation with God and to unlimited transfusions of grace.

14

The Love of the Cross

Mark and Matthew include in their gospels only one saying from the cross, the one which Jesus made his own, one in which his trust in God and the divine love triumphed over both the physical and spiritual pain of the cross. Our meditation on that saying (see Chapter 13) tried to enter into the depth of what was going on in our Lord's heart, and into its personal relevance to ourselves.

Luke and John in their gospels each record three other sayings, John from his own memory of standing by the cross, and Luke from the careful inquiries from eyewitnesses, which he undertook for himself and his Gentile friends (1:1–4). The birth narratives could only have come from our Lord's mother in the first place, and possibly Luke elicited from her also some precious memories of the last hours of the earthly life of Jesus.

We have already meditated in Chapter 11 on the prayer of Jesus in the earliest minutes on the cross, in which he prayed for forgiveness for all who had taken some part in bringing him there, a prayer breathing both love and forgiveness. Luke then tells of a conversation in which all three men hanging on their crosses took part. The two criminals as well as Jesus had heard the jeering of the rulers. One of them turned his head and joined in the mocking. 'If you are the Christ, save yourself and us!' The other, perhaps moved by the first prayer of Jesus, while he and his fellow criminal had been shouting in their agony, realises that it is their own actions that have brought them there, reproves him. Then looking at the inscription over the head of Jesus, he grimly thinks of what a kingdom this is, and now talks directly to the man hanging beneath Pilate's accusing inscription: 'Jesus, remember me, when you come into your kingship.' Jesus replies, 'Today, you will be with me in Paradise.'

'Today' . . . immediately; 'with me' . . . in continuing company; 'in Paradise' . . . the realm of the dead. Faith and love combine in this reply: trust in God and friendliness to man. The other thief must have heard this reply, but Luke could not know what went on in his mind. Nor indeed can anyone writing about it today. But from all that we know of Jesus we can be sure that he had compassion for the hardened thief as well as for the penitent one, with the conviction that before sunset on that day all three would be together in the kingdom of the dead, where Jesus would be much more at home than the other two.

John's Gospel has the word of love spoken to his mother. She with her own sister, and Mary the wife of Cleopas, Mary Magdalene, and the beloved disciple, had found their way to the foot of the cross, and stood in helpless grief for Jesus, hoping that their love would somehow comfort him in his pain. Jesus's love for his mother rises above his pain and he wonders who can take care of her in the future when he is no longer there in physical presence. Then his eyes turn to the beloved and loving disciple and his question is answered. Head and eyes turn to his mother again in love, 'Mother, there is your son', and a further turn of the head, back to John, 'There is your mother.'

The gospel adds that 'from that hour the disciple took her to his own home'. William Temple interprets, 'And that disciple at once leads her away from the scene of suffering . . . he returns "to hear the last words and to see the wondrous end".'[1] I cannot picture Mary consenting to be led away at that moment, and feel that Michaelangelo was nearer the truth in his sculpture in St Peter's, Rome, before which streams of pilgrims stand in silence every day, of Mary holding the dead body across her knees, his head cradled once again in her arms.

[1] *Readings in St John's Gospel*, 2 vols. (London 1939, 1940).

The evangelist may mean that at that very moment the beloved disciple accepted the care laid upon him by the dying Jesus. Later, after the entombment, I can picture his arm around her as he led her back to the upper room for a sad sabbath.

The love shown on the cross was the ultimate, the uttermost, the never-failing love in the life of Jesus, as John tells us, 'having loved his own who were in the world, he loved them to the end'. Questioned by an expert in the study of the law as to its greatest commandment, Jesus had replied that to love God stood first, and to love one's neighbour next. Love was to be universal, it was even to embrace enemies. The love he wanted his disciples to have was to love as he loved, a new and last command.

John came to see that love is the very essence of the Godhead, and that when we love we move from a state of spiritual death into deathless life, into an entirely new country, a kingdom with its own laws. Paul learnt that the most eloquent preaching, intellectual understanding, absolute faith, most generous giving, even martyrdom itself, without love is worth nothing in the eternal scale of values. Down the centuries holy men and women have experienced the love of Christ and crystallised it in words that go straight to the heart. I have found this in a sentence that comes from the earliest known devotional book in English,[2] 'He is not to be gotten or holden by thought but only by love.'

The great Spanish mystic of the sixteenth century, John of the Cross, sends another heart-piercing arrow down the years, 'Where there is no love, pour love in, and you will draw love out.' Samuel Crossman (1624–83) speaks of 'love to the loveless shown, that they might love-ly be'.

The translators of the works of Teilhard de Chardin, a saintly Jesuit of our own century, tried to find an English word which would catch the spirit of the French word which he used to describe the divine, outpouring, permeating love, and finally came up with 'amorising', making everything lovable. An

[2] *The Cloud of Unknowing*, author unknown.

anecdote from a mystery story stays in my memory. Two detectives are talking together about a young tough being sought for murder who is being protected by an elderly aunt.

'I know it' [says one to the other], 'she'll forgive him without question, whatever he has done to her and however high we hang him. It's no use you blaming her, she can't help herself. She's only a vehicle. That's Disinterested Love, chum, a force like nuclear energy. It's absolute.'[3]

In our present troubled years we are learning that love is imperative, and that without it people go wrong. Small children who are not surrounded by love in their earliest years suffer from this deficiency all their lives. Many when they come to what we call 'years of discretion', meaning freedom to choose and decide, leave home, perhaps sub-consciously seeking what they feel they have never had. This loss may accompany them through later years, leading them to homelessness, finding temporary relief, as they think, in drink or drugs, ending in despair; or more hopefully to the social worker, probation officer, psychiatrist who helps to discover the cause of their lostness over a long time of probing, at considerable expense; or to a prison chaplain, prison visitor, a therapy group or a friend to whom they can confide their sorrows and failures; or a priest who in a loving pastoral heart, as well as with the authority entrusted to him by the Church, the corporate continuation of Christ's love, can help them to believe that there is forgiveness for the past and grace for the future and love for the present.

Arising from this conviction of the imperative need of love in early years, we are being led to realise the importance of the nine months of pregnancy, for husbands as well as wives, in the creation of a new life. The histologists' discovery of the pairing of physical chromosomes and genes suggests that there

[3] Margery Allingham, *Hide my Eyes* (London 1958).

are spiritual chromosomes, chromosomes of character which are transmitted to the child being created.

We are being led further back still, by the increasing number of broken marriages, to realise that sexual competence is not enough to ensure lasting happiness. When love is dead, true marriage has died also. Husband and wife need the inter-penetration of spirits as well as of bodies. A verse from a hymn by Jan Struther, the writer who put so much of herself into 'Mrs Miniver', has been an inspiration to me in my own marriage, as well as a prayer when I take part in marriage services as offici-ating priest or as rejoicing friend:

Godhead in human guise
   Once to earth returning,
Daily through human eyes
   Joys of earth discerning:
Grant that we may treasure less
Passion than true tenderness,
   Yet never, Lord, despise
      Heart to sweetheart turning.
     Bless us, God of loving.[4]

These are very contemporary and pragmatic thoughts, impreg-nated, I hope, with the presence of the risen Christ as well as the crucified Christ, leading me to the conviction that his life, ministry, death, survival and universal presence crystallise in simple words, 'Jesus was and is God in a human heart', supremely disclosed in the cross, with the eternal intention of universal incarnation and universal love.

In some moods and in the experience of many people there comes the temptation to feel unloved, and the humbling realis-ation of the poverty of our love for God and our fellow humans. How do we learn to love? The apostle John comes to my rescue once more, when he says, 'We love him because he first loved

[4] *Songs of Praise*, 282.

us.' We learn to love by being loved. All we have to do is to respond to that love and reproduce it.

15

The Great Moment

Mark, Matthew and Luke record in their gospels that Jesus just before he died uttered a loud cry. John (19:30) tells us what it was: 'It is finished!', adding that after Jesus had shouted this, 'he bowed his head and gave up his spirit'. There have been differing interpretations of this sixth utterance on the cross. Some have thought that it was a cry of relief that death was near and that the awful physical suffering of crucifixion was at an end. One can well believe that there was truth in this. Six hours on the cross, preceded by the spiritual struggle in Gethsemane, the misinterpretation of Judas, the offended and hurt spirit of Peter, cross-examinations through the night, the scourging, the mockery of Herod's court and Pilate's soldiers, the purple robe and the crown of thorns, the dragging of the heavy cross beam from Gabbatha to Calvary, mercifully relieved after several falls by Simon of Cyrene, the nailing, the jolting of his limbs as the cross is raised in its socket, and the dragging of the weight of his body on his shoulders and arms. All that is now past, and the tortured body relaxes in preparation for death. Thank God, thank God, that all that suffering is over.

A few interpreters have suggested that this loud cry was one of despair, in a sense of failure. For myself I cannot think so, for Jesus had dealt with this in Gethsemane and had rejected it. Also, had it been so, it would not have been expressed in a loud shout, but in something approaching a whimper. Every Good Friday I find myself more and more disturbed by the Scripture reading from the book of Lamentations, with a verse in which its writer pictures Jerusalem, lamenting over its destruction and forsaken condition: 'Is it nothing to you, all you who pass by? Look and see if there is any sorrow like my sorrow which was brought upon me, which the Lord inflicted on me in the day of his fierce anger' (1:12). I cannot bring myself to say after such a reading, 'This is the word of the Lord', for it seems entirely against Jesus's acceptance of the cross and his whole understanding of the Father's purpose and will, while its assumption of infliction by God in his fierce anger amounts to blasphemy. But that troubling verse was written before Jesus; after Jesus such assumptions are no longer valid or possible.

What then can we think? My answer would be that it is a cry of triumph in the completion of the task which God has laid upon him. Paul puts it for us in a few very clear words, 'God was in Christ, reconciling the world to himself' (2 Cor. 5:19) throughout the years of the ministry, indeed throughout his whole life, and supremely in the cross.

For the first time in religious history a man had been one in heart and mind with the Father, and completely obedient to God. Because of his union with the Father and his full humanity the eternal love and grace of God could flow through him into the whole of humanity. William Temple has summed it up for me in a sentence, 'The date of the triumph of love is Good Friday not Easter Day.'[1] Whenever I conduct meditations on Good Friday I like to include two verses usually kept for Easter day:

The strife is o'er, the battle done;
Now is the Victor's triumph won;
O let the song of praise be sung.
    Hallel-lu-jah!

Death's mightiest powers have done their worst,
And Jesus hath his foes dispersed;
Let shouts of praise and joy outburst.
    Hallel-lu-jah![2]

[1] *Readings in St John's Gospel*, 2 vols. (London 1939, 1940).
[2] *English Hymnal*, 625.

Having uttered that great shout of triumph the gospels tell us that Jesus bowed his head and gave up his spirit to God. Luke alone tells us of his last words, 'Father, into thy hands I commend my spirit', quiet words of loving trust which I imagine only those near the cross heard, John and the weeping women, the centurion and the waiting soldiers. The reader in church services and the individual Christian as he comes to this point instinctively pauses in awed silence, imagination ceases, no words can express the wonder of this great moment.

It is only later that the mind begins to glimpse its significance; global, personal, and eternal. At that moment Jesus gives his spirit into the Father's hands, as indeed he has done all his life. In that one moment death, resurrection, ascension and the release of his spirit to be omnipresent with God, occur simultaneously. The eternal Spirit is everywhere, in the created world, in the kingdom of the dead, even in the hells of spiritual torment in which souls ignorant of the divine love and forgiveness still imprison themselves. Good Friday, Easter day, Ascension day and Pentecost are simultaneous in that one moment. Matthew in his Gospel sees what it all means:

And behold, the curtain of the temple was torn in two, from top to bottom; and the earth shook, and the rocks were split; the tombs also were opened, and many bodies of the saints who had fallen asleep were raised, and coming out of the tombs after his resurrection they went into the holy city and appeared to many. (Matt. 27:51–3).

Paul Tillich, one of the deepest theologians of our century, interprets Matthew's symbolism for us. I summarise his words:

With the insight of a prophet and the skill of an artist the writer of the first gospel describes a series of symbolic events connected with the death of Christ. The sun veils its face in shame for the evil which caused the cross. The curtain of the temple is rent, signifying that the way to God is now open to everybody. The earth is shaken and judged and is no longer the cave of death. The dead are raised because one man has committed his spirit into his Father's hands. Nature has received another meaning; history is transformed; you and I are no longer what we were before.

We humans can only think of God in human terms, and I have dared to write:

Surely, here by the cross
with the limp body hanging there
there must have sounded
the voice from heaven
   once more:
      'Thou art my beloved Son,
        with thee I am well pleased.'
      Son in call,
      Son in obedience,
      Son in love,
      Son in death
        and in triumphant life:
      'My Son, my own dear Son,
      Jesus of Nazareth.
      My Son! My Son!'

The centurion in charge of the execution must have heard all the sayings from the cross, and watched all that happened there. He had probably been present at many crucifixions and never witnessed one quite like this. Luke is probably nearest to what the centurion sadly remarked as he looked at the dead body. 'Certainly this was a righteous man', not meriting such a painful end. Mark, followed by Matthew, during thirty years or more has come to a personal faith and devotion, when he reports the comment of the centurion as, 'Truly, this man was the Son of God', a confession of faith which Christians have made all down the ages and which we, meditating on the passion and cross today, gladly, thankfully and lovingly make with him.

The hours left on that first Good Friday before the sabbath and festival began must have been very painful and anxious for the little group gathered at the foot of the cross. The Jerusalem Jewish authorities, anxious to keep the law's regulations that corpses should not remain on the cross over the sabbath, asked the Governor that death should be hastened for the three on their crosses. Pilate doubtless would have been quite satisfied to leave the bodies exposed, to show how Rome treated criminals and possible leaders of revolt, nevertheless he agreed to their request. So the legs of the two thieves were broken with a heavy mallet, resulting in quick death. When the soldiers came to Jesus and found that he was already dead they did not break his legs, but to make sure, they thrust a spear to his heart. We can imagine the group of Jesus's friends being deeply grieved at this desecration.

Pilate too must have been impressed by the request of two leading rulers, Joseph of Arimathea and Nicodemus, to allow them to bury the body of Jesus. So the nails were drawn and the body taken down by John and the two others, while the weeping women received it into loving hands. In the gospel accounts of this incident there is no hint of a belief in the resurrection. For them the worst has happened, they are left without hope. All that remains are memories and love.

The body is carried to a garden nearby, and laid in a tomb which Joseph had probably prepared for himself and his family. John concludes his memory of that evening with a sad verse that seems final, 'so because of the Jewish day of preparation, as the tomb was close at hand, they laid Jesus there'. In the spiritual world things hidden from the physical eye are already taking place, and a hallelujah chorus is being sung.

16

The Effectiveness of the Cross

We have meditated together on the tension in the heart of Jesus caused by the meeting with a group of Greeks (see Chapter 6) a day or two before the Passover which was finally resolved in the great saying, 'I, when I am lifted up from the earth, will draw all men to myself.' He had only been on the cross a short while when this conviction and promise began to be fulfilled. What was happening in the penitent thief, his realisation that his own actions had brought him to his cross, his realisation that Jesus had done nothing amiss to bring him there, his acceptance of the comfort and company of Jesus, not only on the cross, but in death and beyond, was the first victory of the cross. Had Jesus not been crucified with him, he would have died without companionship and hope.

The verdict of the Roman centurion in charge of the triple execution, who had not met Jesus before and could only judge by the bearing of Jesus and the words spoken during the six hours of physical agony, was a second and immediate effect of the cross. The memory of that six hours acquaintance would stay with him all his life, and perhaps the remembrance of the words to the thief would come to his mind when his own death drew near.

The news that Jesus was being crucified made two of the rulers come out into open discipleship. Neither Joseph of Arimathea nor Nicodemus had been a party to the condemnation of Jesus by the Sanhedrin. Possibly each now felt that he might have spoken out more strongly against it. Nicodemus would certainly have remembered that evening on the housetop when he and Jesus had talked together about the kingdom of God and the need of a change amounting to a new birth before anyone could enter it. Perhaps the two got together before Jesus died, and agreed that while Joseph went to the Governor, Nicodemus would hastily prepare the mixture of aloes and myrrh for anointing the corpse before the sabbath sunset. Visitors to the ruined abbey at Glastonbury would never have wondered at the flowering thorn which legend says Joseph brought to England, if the cross had never happened.

It was a tremendous happening at the next great pilgrimage festival of Pentecost, where three thousand converts were baptised, and Peter's courageous preaching redeemed his failure in the house of Caiaphas. Among that number there would have been Jerusalem Jews who had been present at the crucifixion and deplored it. There would also have been Jews from different parts of the Middle East, who had come to Jerusalem to keep the early harvest festival and the commemoration of the giving of the law. A few days after Pentecost they would be travelling back to their homes to tell others of the wonderful experiences they had had at that festival in Jerusalem.

Peter and his eleven fellow-apostles would know that there were now fellow-disciples in the countries mentioned by Luke in Acts (2:5–13), to whom they could go when they set out on the world mission Jesus had commanded them, much as Paul did in his missionary journeys when he first went to the synagogues of the Jewish Dispersion. Luke in two passages describes the mutual love and care of the new community, their daily worship in the temple, their sharing of everything in common, and their consciousness that the Lord was present with them, so that remarkable things were happening, not only comparable to the things Jesus did in his ministry, but even greater things (Acts 2:42–7, 4:33–5; John 1:50, 5:20, 14:12). Any group of Christians, any congregation, any parochial church council, any synod, wishing to live in the spirit of these first Christians could well spend a whole day or more studying and meditating upon the five passages just mentioned, and relating them to their own neighbourhood.

We can see the influence of the cross in the life and death of Stephen, in his defence before the High Priest's council that was trying him, his realisation that even social and religious customs would have to change in the impact of Jesus, and also when the stones were raining down upon him; and more particularly in his vision of the risen Lord standing at the right hand of God, and his last words, 'Lord, lay not this sin to their charge', so reminiscent of our Lord's first prayer from the cross (Acts 6:11–14, 7:55–60).

Stephen's martyrdom and Christ-like imitation were a human and secondary cause of what many Christians consider to be the greatest happening in the Apostolic Age, the conversion of Saul the Pharisee. He found it impossible to believe that the Messiah could be one who was crucified. He was present at Stephen's stoning and approved of it, though he took no active part in it. From that day on he became the leader of the persecution of these heretical believers in Jesus, not only in Jerusalem and Judaea and Samaria, but as far as Damascus. The memory of Stephen's death must have raised within him the question, 'Suppose these followers of Jesus are right?' To stifle such troubling doubts he went off to Damascus to deal with Christ-believers there. Before he reached Damascus, something exploded within him, as he later said that a blinding light from heaven shone within and around him, and as he lay on the ground a voice said to him, 'Saul, Saul, why do you persecute me?' Trembling and apprehensive he asked, 'Who are you, Lord?', only to hear the voice continuing, 'I am Jesus of Nazareth whom you are persecuting' (Acts 9:1–5). Then came the moment of conversion when he asked, 'What shall I do, Lord?' Meditation on that question leads every Christian to realise that when one asks it in humble sincerity, one's conversion has begun.

The persecutor becomes the persecuted, willing to suffer many things for his new Lord and Master. The proud Pharisee becomes the servant of the Nazarene, an apostle ready to be sent anywhere. On his journey to Rome as a prisoner he comforts the panic-stricken sailors and soldiers on the worst night of the storm, telling them, 'For there stood by me this night an angel of God, whose I am, and whom I serve' (Acts 27:23 AV), seven one-syllable words which speak of a great devotion. In his time there would have been few more-travelled persons. He knew the world more than Jesus did, who had only visited what we now call Lebanon and Jordan and then for short visits only. Saul had been a student under a distinguished rabbi, and a citizen of Tarsus (no mean city, he calls it). He could claim the protection of the Roman Empire, as one of its citizens. He had a view of the world and a vision of its future, which he expressed in his letter to the churches around Ephesus, that God's purpose was 'to gather into one all things in Christ, both earthly and heavenly'. Very few people would say that their chief impression of Paul was that of a very loving and lovable man, yet under the influence of the crucified and risen Jesus he wrote the greatest hymn of love, that will move people as long as this world lasts, and indeed beyond human history. Paul was one of the greatest victories of the cross.

All down the centuries there have been men and women who were prepared to suffer torture and death rather than deny Jesus as their Lord and Saviour. In our own century we see the magnetic, inspiring love of the cross in people like Edith Cavell, Dietrich Bonhoeffer, Teilhard de Chardin, Archbishop Lewom, Martin Luther King, Mother Teresa, Leonard Cheshire and Sue Ryder. We thank God too for Bishop Tutu and his dedication to change in racial relationships, without acts of violence.

During the Second World War some of my friends in Burma underwent torture, inspired and sustained by the memory of Christ on the cross. Two Burman priests were several times strung up by their hands to the roof beams of their prisons and beaten. When Burma was liberated they both told me that the thing that kept them free from despair and resentment was the thought of Christ being scourged, and his prayer for those who had any part in bringing him to the cross. A third priest, who had been trained in the College of Holy Cross in Rangoon while I was warden found himself the only priest in a large area in central Burma, and spent the three years of occupation going faithfully round a dozen towns and villages ministering the sacraments, watched with suspicious eyes by the military.

My most grateful memory of the war in Burma is of the Burmese headmistress of a teachers' training college in Rangoon, of which I was the chaplain. Her name was Ma Pwa Sein. When war broke out and Burma was invaded she took her students off to what we both hoped would be a safe place to carry on their training. However, a band of pro-Japanese dacoits arrived at this Karen village, burnt the houses down and rounded up the villagers nearly all of whom were Christians. The people of Nyaung-ngu had previously sheltered two British soldiers, lost and exhausted, who had somehow been cut off from their regiment. The leader of the nationalist group ordered all Karens to gather on one side and any Burmans on the other. Ma Pwa Sein was the only Burman, and when the troop attacked the larger body of villagers, cutting them to pieces with their large dahs (knives), she walked back into the rest and died with them. The account of the massacre was told to me after the war, by two villagers who had managed to hide in the bamboos surrounding the village.

Ma Pwa Sein's name is included in the list of modern martyrs commemorated in a memorial chapel of St Paul's Cathedral, which has the following dedication inscription:

In this chapel we commemorate the modern martyrs, those who since 1850 witnessed to Christ and suffered death rather than renounce him. The names of such heroes of the faith are so numerous that we have confined our roll of honour to those of the Anglican Communion, and even so our record is imperfect, for many have died for Christ whose names are unknown to us, though not forgotten by God. We have made this memorial to commemorate those who have fought already, and to train those who shall fight hereafter.

All the churches will have martyrs who died for their faith, and as the inscription in St Paul's implies, they form a veritable army, well meriting the verse in the Te Deum, 'The white robed army of martyrs praise Thee', scores of thousands from the undivided Church and many more from the churches in separation. The Roman Church alone, whose members make up half of the total number of Christians in the world, have enough names to line the walls of Westminster Cathedral. The numberless total of such martyrs is a fulfilment of our Lord's faith and promise of the continuous drawing power of his death on the cross.

The continued existence of the Christian Church is further evidence of the power of the cross. Today Christians number a thousand million people of every country, race and colour, almost a quarter of the world's population. They have become disciples of Jesus Christ, not because of the Sermon on the Mount, magnificent anthology of moral teaching for the life of disciples though it is, nor because of our Lord's healing miracles, full of compassion as they are. It is the love revealed in the cross and the salvation that has come to so many through it. We speak of the Church as the collective body of Christ, through which he acts today; in the Nicene Creed we confess what it is in the will of Christ and what ought to be its cardinal characteristics – one, holy, catholic in truth and love, apostolic in its sense of mission to the world. We long and pray that it may have these marks in all its members and in all its branches. Every priest and minister of the Church knows holy, humble and loving souls, all of them unknown saints, known only by God, all of them drawn to God by the magnet of the cross.

There are still many victories to be won. The unity of the Church for which Christ prayed in his great high-priestly prayer before he and his disciples left the upper room for Gethsemane, on the last night of his incarnate life, still remains an obstacle to winning the world to its Creator and Redeemer. This long delayed unity prevents the Church from speaking with one voice about the pressing issues of each age, and the new order of society which is imperative in an age of new technology, with its problems of employment, leisure, and the development of under-nourished nations in a world of wealth and plenty, so that people everywhere may have the abundant life of God's will. The abolition of war, universally accepted disarmament, the right use of nuclear energy to lift the burdens of so many people in every country, are other victories still to be won. More personally, the death of Christ and his interpretation of it as going to the eternal Father, should release us from the fear of death.

We who profess to be Christ's disciples believe that God revealed himself in Christ, in human terms that all humans can understand. We believe that God is the Creator and Father of us all, the Redeemer of us all, that he wills to incarnate himself in each one of us. We believe that in the cross God showed us his heart, the sacred heart, the eternal heart that never ceases to love and forgive, whatever we do to him and his Christ. If we really believe all that, we must surely believe that God is at work among all, starting where they are. We must be interested in the spiritual nature and experience of people of other faith. We have no monopoly of God and Christ. We must not dismiss others as heathen and pagan. On the cross Christ died for all, and everyone we meet is equally a brother or a sister for whom Christ died, whatever may be his or her religious tradition or cultural milieu.

I can never be grateful enough to Cardinal Bea, the head of the Secretariat for Christian Unity, who at a meeting in Rome in January 1962 of Christians of all churches, Jews, Muslims, and people of other creeds, declared:

> Perhaps few among you have had so many dealings with men of different races, different religions, different beliefs and different cultures as I – unworthily – have. In all these dealings I have always found a great love, a wide-open heart, always opens the hearts of others. This great love must be not mere diplomacy but the result of a sincere conviction that we are all the children of the one God, who has created mankind, who has created each one of us, and whose children we all are.

'A great love and a wide-open heart' – that was Christ on the cross and that must be our attitude to people of other faith or none.

Muslims do not believe that Christ died on the cross, they cannot think that God would let down one of his prophets by allowing such a fate to happen. Either Christ was not dead but taken down from the cross and revived or someone else was crucified in his place. In spite of this a Muslim teacher, Al-Hallaj, who was crucified for his supposedly heretical views, when he saw the cross and the nails, turned to the people and uttered a prayer ending with the words:

> And these thy servants who are gathered to slay me, in zeal for Thy religion and in desire to win Thy favour, forgive them, O Lord, and have mercy upon them, for verily if Thou hadst revealed to them that which Thou hast revealed to me, they would not have done what they have done; and if Thou hadst hidden from me that which Thou hast hidden from them, I should not have suffered this tribulation. Glory unto Thee in whatsoever Thou willest.[1]

Al-Hallaj died a Muslim, yet one cannot help thinking he knew something of the New Testament account of Jesus on the cross.

As I meditate and write, I recall what I heard a Jewish rabbi friend say. At a meeting of Christians in Jerusalem, the Professor of New Testament Studies in the Hebrew University there remarked that he prayed for Christians every day. When the time came for discussion the first question asked was, 'What do you pray for us Christians?' His reply reduced his audience to silence. 'I pray', he said, 'that you Christians may be more like your Jesus.'

Another rabbi friend, Pinchas Lapide, in a discussion on German radio with Hans Kung about their respective faiths, said in his final remark something to this effect: 'If when Jesus

[1] R. A. Nicholson, *The Mystics of Islam* (London 1914).

returns he turns out to be the Messiah, I shall be only too pleased.'

It will be a great day when Jews, Christians and Muslims can get together as fellow seekers, fellow believers in God, fellow worshippers of him, and tell one another of their experiences of him, not evading their differences. It is beginning to happen at a deep level at the Interfaith Research department, at the central headquarters of the Selly Oak colleges in Birmingham.

This meditation began in the remembrance of the great moment when Jesus died on the cross; it has taken us far in time and place and memory. It will take writer and reader into deeper understanding and devotion, as each continues it in a stilled mind, a listening ear, a wide-open heart.

17

The Risen Lord

All four gospel writers are silent about the day and a half that followed the death of Jesus. We can well imagine the sad thoughts and memories of his closest friends and disciples, and the pilgrims from Galilee who had shouted 'hosanna' a week before. Matthew, however, tells us of a fear in the minds of some of the rulers that Jesus might be risen, a fear that seems stronger in their minds than any hope of resurrection in the minds of his followers. Some of the temple officials even feared that the disciples might steal the body, hide it, and try to believe and declare that he had risen from the dead, regardless of the difficulty, then as now, of disposing of a dead body. The enemies of Jesus would certainly have made every effort to discover his body and put it on public display.

Matthew is always thinking of the spiritual significance, of divine interventions in the spiritual enveloping of human activities. He can only describe these in human terms. At the request of the Jewish rulers, there is permission to set a guard over the tomb, the great round stone closing the entrance to the tomb is sealed. Every human precaution has been taken, none of which can defeat the divine activity, symbolised by an earthquake, the rolling away of the stone, the flashing brilliance of a spiritual figure, and the quake of fear in the guards. The reality behind the symbolic signs is that nothing can avert or defeat the fact of the living Jesus, not liquidated by physical death, but still present in a spiritual way which will not be limited by a flesh-and-blood body, and will be perceivable by those with spiritual eyesight.

So we come to the experiences of the first Easter day,

commemorating the perception of what had happened at the great moment when Jesus died. 'Three days' seems to be a symbolic length of time, expressing the interval between some great spiritual event and the human perception of its significance. Something of that kind may have been in the mind of the prophet Hosea when, thinking of the sufferings of the northern kingdom and Judah, he appeals to both, 'Come, let us return to the Lord; for he has torn that he may heal', and adds, 'After two days he will revive us; on the third day he will raise us up that we may live before him' (6:1–2).

'On the third day' then, the first day of the week, the faithful women are on the way to the tomb while it is barely light, to complete the embalming of the body of Jesus. To their surprise they find the great stone rolled away and the tomb empty. As they stand round in puzzled amazement, a voice comes, whether speaking in a way that would be audible to any outsider or in an intuitional way in each heart, it is difficult to say. The voice asks, 'Why do you seek the living among the dead?' They then remember how Jesus had told them several times before his death that God would raise him up, and decide to go and tell Peter and the other disciples that he would go before them to Galilee and they would meet him there. As they move in faith to do this, the realisation comes to them, 'He is not here, he is risen.' As they hurry to do this, Matthew tells us that they experience the risen Lord with them, and fall to their knees in joy and worship.

Mark in his Gospel says that the women, in spite of their vision of a young man arrayed in white and his message, 'he is risen; he is not here', fled from the tomb trembling and astonished, 'and they said nothing to anyone, for they were afraid' (16:8), perhaps shaken at the amazing conviction that was dawning in their hearts. At this point Mark's Gospel, as in the manuscripts that scholars think of as the earliest and most authoritative, breaks off, and the passage 16:9–20 is only seen in later texts and versions, giving the impression of a later summary from the other three gospels. There has been much discussion about what is spoken of as the lost ending of Mark.

102

It might have ended with verse 8, which certainly conveys a sense of mystery, and of a tremendous revelation of almost unbelievable truth. When they got back to the apostles and recounted their experience at the tomb and on their way back, they were received with scepticism. Luke tells us that their words 'seemed to them an idle tale, and they did not believe them'. It all seemed too good to be true.

According to Luke, Mary Magdalene was one of the women in this early visit to the tomb. According to John she had no early experience of the risen Lord for she ran to where Peter and John were staying and grievingly announced, 'They have taken away the Lord out of the tomb, and we do not know where they have laid him.' At this shattering news Peter and John run towards the tomb. The younger man outruns Peter, looks down into the well of the tomb and sees the discarded grave clothes. Peter, breathless, arrives a moment later and rushes into the empty tomb, followed by John. The empty grave clothes seem evidence that the resurrection was not a purely physical thing. If it had been, it is hardly likely that the risen Jesus would have left it naked. The writer of the fourth gospel says John then saw and believed – the amazing transformation that had taken place, a great spiritual happening which convinced him, which Peter some time later would experience, and for which some years later he would thank and bless God: 'Blessed be the God and Father of our Lord Jesus Christ! By his great mercy we have been born anew to a living hope through the resurrection of Jesus Christ from the dead' (1 Pet. 1:3).

Mary Magdalene, still hopeless in her grief, returns to the tomb, weeping and wondering wherever those who have taken the body could have hidden it. Suddenly she is conscious of a presence beside her whom she mistakes for the gardener. Evidently she had no idea that it could be Jesus; even when he speaks, asking her why she is weeping, she does not recognise him, and says that if he will tell her where he has laid the Lord's body, she will take it away. The risen Jesus must have chuckled as he addressed her by name as he had done many times before – 'Ma-a-ry!' Now she does recognise him and replies, 'My Master, my Rabbi!' The old familiar King James version represents Jesus as then saying, 'Touch me not' (John 20:17 AV), which has puzzled me as well as many others. The modern versions make clear our Lord's reply, 'Don't hold me, for I have not yet ascended to the Father' (RSV). Mary Magdalene wanted nothing more than the old relationship before he was crucified. Jesus is saying in effect, 'Do not keep me earthbound, for I am ascending to the Father.' She is to tell the disciples whom he now calls brethren, that he is ascending 'to my Father and your Father, to my God and your God'. A new era has dawned; it is to the advantage of them all that he should be with the Father, as he had said in his last charge to them in the upper room.

That same afternoon two disciples were walking out to the village of Emmaus, about seven miles from Jerusalem. One of them was named Cleopas. Artists and commentators all assume that the other was a male disciple also. But it could well have been the wife of Cleopas, who had stood forty-eight hours earlier with the little group at the foot of the cross. They were talking together about what had happened, and from the conversation it is clear that they had the same worldly ideas of our Lord's messiahship as the twelve apostles. As they walked and talked Jesus drew near and walked and talked with them, but they did not recognise him. They told him of what had happened in Jerusalem, and how their hopes had been disappointed. They also told of how some women of their company had been early at the tomb that morning, who had returned saying they had seen a vision of angels who said that Jesus was alive, although they did not see him. He then gently reproved them for their mistaken ideas about the Messiah and pointed out to them his own interpretation of messianic texts in the Scriptures. Still they did not recognise him.

Arrived at Emmaus they pressed this companion, who had so strangely warmed their heart, to stay the night with them. Their words of invitation are among the best loved texts of the New Testament: 'Stay with us, for it is toward evening and the day is far spent' (Luke 24:29), words that can be used not only in the evening of the day, the evening of life but also the evening of the world when Christians think of the consummation of creation and the history of the world.

When the meal has been prepared and they sit down at the table, the supposed stranger takes the loaf of bread, breaks it and says over it the usual Jewish blessing of God, as he had done so often when they shared a meal before. Immediately their eyes are opened and they recognise him, and 'he vanishes out of their sight'. It must have been dark by this time, for the sun sets early in Palestine compared with sunset in western countries. In spite of a dark journey back they set off for Jerusalem to tell the eleven disciples of their experience, only to find that the risen Lord has been with them also and in addition has appeared to Peter.

They add that the risen Lord made himself known to them in the breaking of bread, another much-loved text from what is to many the loveliest of all the resurrection narratives, verified in the Christian's experience of the Eucharist, and in the consciousness of what many speak of as 'the real presence'.

John's Gospel (20:19–20) tells us more about this meeting. The ten disciples meet behind barred doors, afraid that the Jewish authorities may want to arrest them also. Suddenly they are conscious of the presence of Jesus with them. Barred doors can no longer keep him out. His familiar greeting of 'Shalom, peace be with you' convinces them that it is he indeed. If further proof is needed, they perceive the nail marks in his hands, and the spear thrust to his heart, spiritual identifiable marks he will carry for all eternity.

The victory of the cross, and God's seal in the resurrection and the forgiveness proclaimed throughout the passion together form a gospel to take out to the world, so the mission to the world can begin at once: 'As the Father has sent me, so I send you.' And he breathes into them divine breath to inspire, strengthen and sanctify them (John 20:21–2). What peace and joy and love must have filled their hearts on that first Easter evening!

Thomas was not there at this reunion on the first Easter evening. When he was told of what had happened, he said that he could only believe in the truth of what the others told him if he could put his fingers into the nail marks in the hands, and thrust his hand into the spear wound in the side of Jesus. This was not an unreasonable condition, for the others had been shown the marks of the wounds in that first reunion. The interesting thing to me is that Jesus knew what had been said by Thomas, although he himself was not visibly present. John, writing his Gospel many years later, puts himself in our place, and says that those who do not ask for physical proof but rely on spiritual sight and experience are blessed.

Looking at the various experiences of that day we cannot make a rationalised timetable of them, for the risen Lord is no longer living in our conditions, but in those of eternity, which are not governed by time, space and physical presence as we know them. He can move at will in an instant of time. He does not have to walk back the seven miles from Emmaus to Jerusalem, taking more than two hours on the journey. He is there at will. Being with God he shares the divine omnipresence, and can be in more places than one at any given moment. Nothing can keep him out, no hospital regulations about visiting hours, no prison cells locked up for the night, no solitary confinements and no deathbeds are lonely, no air crashes or terrorisms, or tortures unattended, no mourning heart uncomforted. The risen Lord fulfils his promise, 'Lo, I am with you always, even to the end of time', and beyond.

18

Personal Response to the Cross

It is remarkable that Paul, who in his days as a rabbi was so opposed to the idea of a suffering Messiah, should after his conversion regard the cross as the central point of his faith and teaching. 'I decided to know nothing among you,' he says to the Christians at Corinth, 'except Jesus Christ and him crucified' (1 Cor. 2:2). Writing to his friends in Galatia, the cross has become even more personalised: 'I have been crucified with Christ; it is no longer I who live, but Christ who lives in me, and the life I now live in the flesh I live by faith in the Son of God, who loved me and gave himself for me' (Gal. 2:20).

Something like this must happen to each individual disciple. I must realise that Christ loves me, that he gave himself for me, that from now on I live by faith, letting him inspire and direct me. That seems attractive and not too difficult. It is the first part of Paul's experience that is far more difficult to undergo. Can I say in all truth that I have been crucified with Christ? That in some way I have died, and so begin to live a new kind of life? If I really mean this, it means a new birth. Not only do I have to avoid scandalous sins or be content with respectability, but I have to repudiate selfish living, self-will, self-motivation, self-seeking, self-satisfaction, self-centredness and all the other spiritual sins hyphenated with the word 'self'. For most of us that amounts to something like the cross. Paul said in one of his self-revelatory moments, 'I die daily', which I think meant more than daily dangers. It included a never-ending mortification of self-centredness in any form.

Then, promises Paul, Christ comes to live in me. The risen

107

Christ comes and knocks at the door of the soul, he keeps knocking, and when I hear the knocking and open the door for him to enter, he will not be content with just waiting in the small hall of the front or back door, he will want to enter every other room in the house of the self, doors labelled sex, money, ambition, work, leisure, relationships with others, the attics where we keep the rubbish and the cellars where we bury the things of which we are ashamed. As he knocks at every door and is allowed to enter and see what is there, and then to cleanse and sanctify, his incarnation within us grows.

Angelus Silesius, a German poet and mystic (1624–77) puts it in these simple and moving words:

> Though Christ a thousand times
>   In Bethlehem be born,
> If he's not born in thee
>   Thy soul is still forlorn.
> The cross on Calvary's hill
>   Will never save thy soul;
> The cross in thine own heart
>   Alone can make thee whole.

There will be times when we may have to bear a cross of pain or suffering, some injustice inflicted upon us by others, either in hateful words or perhaps hateful deeds. Then Christ becomes our Simon of Cyrene and carries our cross and ourselves. Another promise is fulfilled, 'come to me, all who labour and are heavy laden, and I will give you rest'.

John Masefield, in his poem, 'The Everlasting Mercy', makes a converted poacher speak of the change in himself brought about by his conversion:

> I did not think, I did not strive,
> The deep peace burnt my me alive;
> The bolted door had broken in,
> I knew that I had done with sin.
> I knew that Christ had given me birth

> To brother all the souls on earth,
> And every bird and every beast
> Should share the crumbs broke at the feast.

The cross and the resurrection are combined in Paul's personalised words to the Galatians.

In his letter to the Christians at Colosse he writes:

> If then you have been raised with Christ, seek those things that are above where Christ is seated at the right hand of God. Set your minds on things that are above, not on things that are on the earth. For you have died, and your life is hid with Christ in God. (Col. 3:1–3)

Here the cross, the resurrection and the ascension are held together, and Paul goes on to list the sins that have to be surrendered, when we have put off the old nature and put on the new nature, which is 'renewed according to the likeness of the Creator' (Col. 3:4–10).

Father Harry Williams stresses the inner freedom from outer compulsion that comes with the new life in Christ:

> To be raised from the dead is to be no longer the prisoner of one's environment. It is to be free from the chains of one's conditioning. It is to realise that it is not necessary to play the game which is being played on us, so that we can play our own game not the one imposed. That is the secret so far unlearnt by those who despitefully use us. They react to life as life has treated them. They are bloody because life is bloody . . . let us be free to be our own master and to live our own life, and not to be merely the sport and toy of circumstance, with everything we do automatically dictated by what is done to us.[1]

Paul gives equal centrality to the resurrection as to the cross.

[1] *True Resurrection* (London 1983).

He lists the original witnesses to it – Peter, the twelve apostles, James, a gathering of five hundred believers many of whom he says were still living when he wrote to the Corinthians. Then he adds, 'Last of all he appeared also to me' (1 Cor. 15:1–11). Every believer all down the centuries and today in every part of the world ought to be able to say the same. Everyone of us should be able to speak of our experience of the risen Christ.

So we can begin to live the resurrection life now. We shall not be automatically guarded against temptation or preserved from failure, but there will be within us a new force of grace and love on which we can draw, and a Companion with us on every step of the journey. If and when we fail, we can go to God and ask his forgiveness, and Christ who expects us to forgive others seventy times seven will go beyond that in his own forgivingness. With forgiveness, and grace on God's part, we shall be able to grow in holiness and love, and so train for the new and eternal order of being which God has prepared for them that love him, and also for those who do not yet do so.

We can never be grateful enough to God for our creation and for all the blessings of life and love, and above all for his inestimable love in the redemption of the world and ourselves by our Lord Jesus Christ, for the means of grace and hope of glory. Isaac Watts, 250 years ago, voiced our love and devotion in his great passiontide hymn:

When I survey the wondrous Cross
   On which the Prince of glory died,
My richest gain I count but loss,
   And pour contempt on all my pride.[2]

There is a further verse, which is often sung at the top of our voices, but the words of it are so tremendous that I feel moved to whisper them and then fall to silent meditation:

[2] *English Hymnal,* 107.

Were the whole realm of nature mine,
   That were a present far too small;
Love so amazing, so divine,
   Demands my soul, my life, my all.

Other words of devotion and thanksgiving often used by me are in a prayer which Eric Milner-White gave us:

> Blessed be thy Name, O Jesu, Son of the most high God; blessed be the sorrow thou sufferedst when thy holy hands and feet were nailed to the tree; and blessed thy love when, the fullness of pain accomplished, thou didst give thy soul into the hands of the Father; so by thy Cross and precious Blood redeeming all the world, all longing souls departed and the numberless unborn; who now livest and reignest in the glory of the eternal Trinity, God for ever and ever.[3]

Our prolonged meditation on the cross and resurrection, Good Friday and Easter day and today, is summed up for us in the closing words of the Epistle to the Hebrews:

> Now may the God of peace who brought again from the dead our Lord Jesus, the great shepherd of the sheep, by the blood of the eternal covenant, equip you with everything good that you may do his will, working in you that which is pleasing in his sight, through Jesus Christ; to whom be glory for ever and ever. Amen. (Heb. 13:20–1)

[3] *A Procession of Passion Prayers* (London 1950).